HISTORY OF ALASKA

THE MACMILLAN COMPANY
NEW YORK . BOSTON . CHICAGO . DALLAS
ATLANTA . SAN FRANCISCO

MACMILLAN & CO., LIMITED
LONDON . BOMBAY . CALCUTTA
MELBOURNE

THE MACMILLAN COMPANY
OF CANADA, LIMITED
TORONTO

ARCTIC
SIBERIA
Wrangell I
Chaun Bay
Kolyuchin Bay
Holy Cross B
East Cape
C Lisburne
Kotzebue Sound
Bering Strait
C Prince of Wales
SEWARD PENINSULA
Nome
Gulf of Anadir
Anadir B
Olintorski Gulf
St Lawrence I
Norton Sound
RUSSIA
UNITED STATES
St Matthew I
Nunivak I
BERING SEA
Pribilof Islands
Attu I
Near Is
Rat Islands
ALEUTIAN ISLANDS
Andreanof Islands
Atka I
Fox Islands
Unimak
Dutch Harbor
Unalaska I
East from Greenwich 180° West from Greenwich

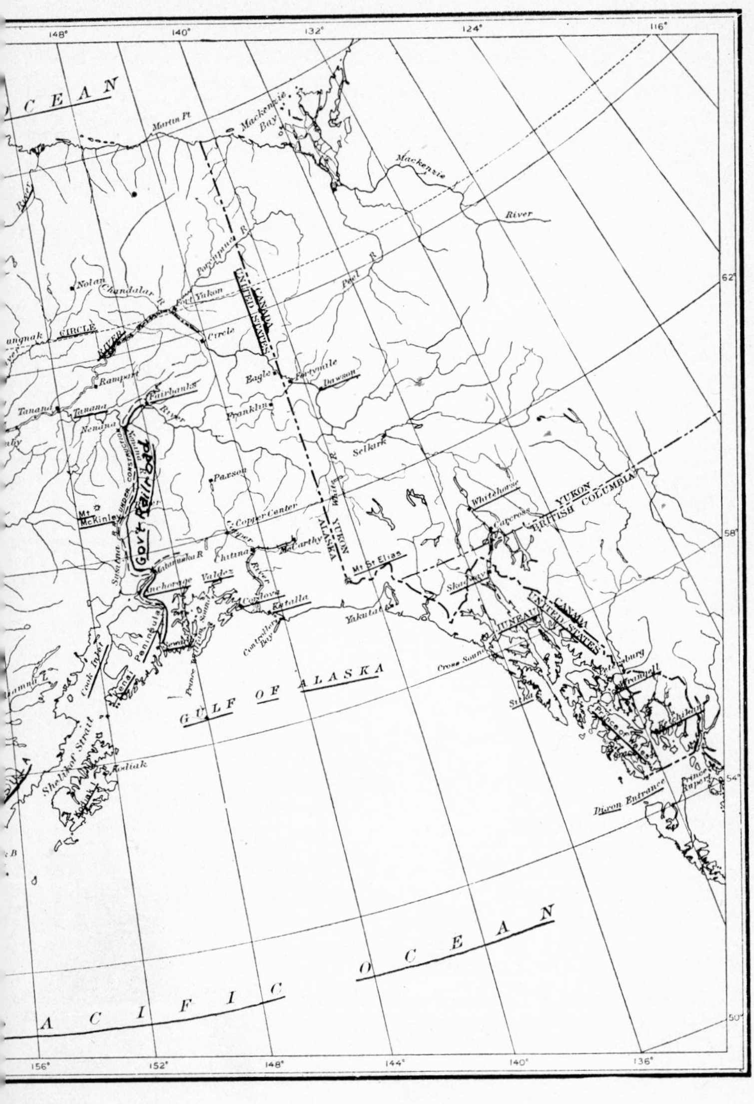

400 500 Miles

400 500 Kilometers

HISTORY OF
ALASKA

BY

HENRY W. CLARK

New York
THE MACMILLAN COMPANY
1930

Set up and printed.
Published April, 1930.

SET UP BY BROWN BROTHERS LINOTYPERS
PRINTED IN THE UNITED STATES OF AMERICA
BY THE CORNWALL PRESS

TO

PROFESSOR EDWARD CHANNING

HARVARD UNIVERSITY

TO WHOSE INSPIRATION, ENCOURAGEMENT, AID AND CRITICISM THIS BOOK OWES WHATEVER OF MERIT IT MAY CONTAIN.

PREFACE

At the outset the reader should know what a perusal of this work will evidence; that is, that this is *a* history of Alaska and not an attempt at *the* history. The book is neither as interpretive nor as exhaustive as I would have liked to have made it. Alaska is still in the infancy of its development and historical research on the subject is just as elementary. This condition is liable to maintain longer than in the instance of most regions because of certain peculiar circumstances.

Russian archives which bulk large in any study of Alaska are a terrific obstacle to surmount, both because of the inaptitude for Americans to acquire facile use of that language, and the disturbed political conditions in that country. Dr. Golder made a vast store of material available during his comparatively short but brilliant period of historical labor, but his unfortunate loss leaves the field again almost a dark continent.

Meanwhile, the need of bringing together and summarizing some of the researches of recent years was felt by many. At the suggestion of Professor Channing and because of his kindly encouragement this task was attempted together with some effort, however slight, toward picturing the people and true perspective of Alaska's place in the world of to-day.

No scholarly, thorough histories of Alaska have been written since the last decade of the last century when the works of Bancroft and Dall were before the public. Such a work is needed now and the recent bibliography by Judge Wickersham will be an invaluable aid in the preparation. Even if I could have afforded the leisure to set such a task for myself, I would not have dared attempt it with my background of study and experience. Professor Channing experienced the need of a modern compilation while investigating the part that Alaska should play in his monumental History of the United States. He was kind enough to suggest this attempt because he felt that my birth and early residence in Alaska, coupled with ten years in New England, would give a fairer perspective than usual.

Throughout the work, I have tried to keep this perspective by avoiding on the one hand the booster spirit and on the other, the spirit of political rancor. Nevertheless, there is a strong temptation to extol Alaska as a natural reaction to the numerous errors that have been circulated about the country; to this, I have succumbed all too often.

As far as possible, the book is a compendium of the valuable research of such scholars as Golder, Stefansson, Andrews, Spicer, Farrand and others, to all of whom tribute is here offered. Further than this, some attempt has been made to link Alaskan history with that of the contemporary world rather than regard its development as an isolated phenomenon. Examples in point are the reigns of Peter the Great and Alexander I in Russia, each of which brought Russian national consciousness and expansion resulting respectively in the discovery by Bering, and the organization of the country under Baranof. In a similar way the Crimean War brought the sale of Alaska; the Spanish-American War altered the course of the Great Gold Rush, and the effect of the World War, though not yet fully ascertainable, was certainly great.

Another angle of Alaskan history which has scarcely been touched in this book, is the influence of the fact that it is the last frontier and free land of the United States. The hatred of absentee rule at Washington, D. C., though often justifiable, is a notable instance, and the failure to recognize the cause of this hatred has discolored many works on Alaska.

I have already intimated some of the obligations that I owe Professor Channing for giving me the opportunity to enjoy the preparation of this book. His kindness has been attested by so many notable scholars that I would presume to do more than enumerate my obligations and let my appreciation be all that I can testify. He has read two drafts of manuscript and the proof, all accompanied with candid, invaluable criticisms. To the Reverend Kashevaroff and the Honorable James W. Wickersham, I owe deepest thanks, and homage to their knowledge of Alaska. I take this inadequate means also of thanking those numerous Alaskans and friends of Alaska whom I have bothered with correspondence during the past four years. Especially among them I would like to single out Joe Ulmer, a real Alaskan sourdough, and Mr. Allen of Seattle. I would have liked to have shown my appreciation to the late Captain Connell, founder of the Arctic Brotherhood, for his story of that event. His son has been my chief reliance for the illustrations contained herein.

I have presumed on the time and patience of many in my work, especially on that of Mr. Wright and Miss Burns at Harvard and my obligations to them mount faster than I can attest. My mother and relatives have been coworkers throughout the preparation of the work.

I am all too conscious of the errors of omission and commission for all of which I can plead the excuse only of a maiden effort. It has been said that all you need ask of your worst enemy, is that he write a book. This effort is offered in the hope that it will be received charitably rather than in that spirit.

No attempt has been made to list a bibliography of the works consulted in the preparation of this book as several excellent bibliographies are now available for students of the subject, the leader among them being the work of Mr. Wickersham already mentioned. The writer has worked chiefly in the Widener Library of Harvard University. The collections in the Boston Public Library, the New York Public Library and the Congressional Library at Washington, D. C., have also been consulted. Much valuable data was obtained from the Western Union library at the company headquarters in New York City. It is my fond hope that some day I will be able to delve further into the subject by exhausting the possibilities of the Pacific Coast libraries.

CONTENTS

PAGE

PREFACE vii

CHAPTER

I. GEOGRAPHY AND CLIMATE 1

II. ETHNOLOGY 22

III. DISCOVERY AND EXPLORATION 32

IV. RUSSIAN OCCUPATION 50

V. PURCHASE OF ALASKA 60

VI. NEGLECT 81

VII. THE "RUSH" ERA 98

VIII. INTERNATIONAL COMPLICATIONS 116

IX. TERRITORIAL GOVERNMENT 129

X. SOCIAL AND INTELLECTUAL GROWTH 142

XI. ECONOMIC DEVELOPMENT 156

XII. MODERN ALASKA 181

INDEX 193

LIST OF ILLUSTRATIONS

Map of Alaska . . . . *Frontispiece*

PAGE

Alaska superimposed on the United States 3

Childs Glacier near Cordova . . . . *Facing* 6

Stand of spruce in Alaska Tongass forest . . . . *Facing* 18

Thlingit dug-out canoe, Wrangell . . . . . . *Facing* 26

Voyages of Deshneff and Bering 37

Route of Bering and Chirikoff 39

Mt. St. Elias and Cape St. Elias . . . . . . *Facing* 42

Voyages of Cook and Vancouver 47

Baranof Castle, Sitka . . . . *Facing* 58

Sitka in the early days of American occupation . . *Facing* 82

U. S. S. "Jamestown," warship which governed Alaska 1879-84 . . . . *Facing* 90

Treadwell Mine in early days . . . . *Facing* 94

S. S. "Portland" arriving in Seattle, Washington, with "ton of gold," June 17, 1897 . . . . *Facing* 102

Stampeders packing up the ice steps of Chilkoot Pass . *Facing* 104

"Soapy" Smith, Alaskan bad man of Klondike rush . *Facing* 106

Nome Beach at height of gold rush and bringing in the mail at Nome . . . . *Facing* 110

Map of boundary dispute 119

Bering Sea, showing how the Aleutian Islands apparently land-lock this sea . . . . *Facing* 126

Bureau control of Alaska 136

"Scotty" Allan and one of his racing teams . . . *Facing* 150

Salmon trap 167

Herd of reindeer in northern Alaska . . . . . *Facing* 178

HISTORY OF ALASKA

HISTORY OF ALASKA

CHAPTER I

GEOGRAPHY AND CLIMATE

GEOGRAPHY and climate play a larger part in the history of Alaska than in that of many other countries. Their importance lies in the great amount of misinformation that has been and still is accepted as fact.

The common fallacies of regarding the Klondike as a part of Alaska, and referring to Alaska as an ice-bound country are examples in point.

The geography of Alaska has loomed large in the history of the country—first, because the long stretching Aleutian Islands afforded easy access to the country from the coasts of Siberia, so easy that the earliest explorers and traders from Russia touched the shores of Alaska in vessels that to-day would not be considered seaworthy enough to venture more than a mile from shore. Having reached Attu, the westernmost island, the visibility of one island with another enabled the exploration and discovery of the country to proceed almost as though by steps throughout the entire archipelago to the mainland. At the same time similiar penetration into the country was rendered easy on the southeast by the so-called Inland Passage, or the island sheltered coast line of the North Pacific Ocean from Puget Sound north for a distance of over a thousand miles. The numerous harbors, anchorages and sheltered waterways made coastwise exploration an easy matter. The mountains immediately behind the coast line acted as a barrier to interior exploration until the discovery of such passes as Chilkoot, Thompson, and the rivers, in the nineteenth century, opened the hinterland. So geography has played its part both in facilitating and in hampering the history of Alaska.

The outstanding surprises to any one approaching the subject of Alaska in a geographical way are the tremendous size of the country and the mild climate. The usual practice of representing Alaska as an appendage on the northwest corner of North America puts the region out of its true proportion. To say that Alaska has an area of about 590,000 square miles, and a coast line of 35,000 miles is by itself surprising, but the startling size of this country is best portrayed by superimposing it upon a map of the United States.

If this were done, Attu Island, at the extreme end of the Aleutian Archipelago, would rest upon California at about Los Angeles, and Dixon Entrance, the southeastern extremity of Alaska, would rest upon Savannah, Georgia. Point Barrow, the northernmost point in Alaska, would be at about Duluth, Minnesota, and the main body of the country would cover six large middle western states between the Dakotas and the Great Lakes, and a half of three others. This area is equal to about one-fifth that of the whole United States. Moreover, the coast line is greater than that of continental United States. The size of the country is further

Comparative Areas—Alaska one-fifth the size of the United States.

brought out by the fact that it has a greater range of climate than that between Florida and Maine. The country covers 20 degrees of latitude and 54 degrees of longitude, the northernmost point being within 18 degrees of the pole, and the southernmost in the same latitude as Liverpool, England. The easternmost point is 2,500 miles from the westernmost.

The geographic position can be appreciated by a comparison with European localities. We notice that Point Barrow is in the same latitude as North Cape, and that Dixon Entrance corresponds to Copenhagen. Thus Alaska is situated similarly to the Scandinavian countries. Sitka, the former capital, is in the same latitude as Edinburgh. This correspondence of localities is favorable to Alaska if we remember that the Alaskan points noted all have a warmer climate than the parallel European points.

The geographical provinces of Alaska correspond exactly with those in the United States if we imagine ourselves approaching the United States from the west or Pacific Coast. Along the coast, including the islands, is the Pacific mountain system from 50 to 200 miles wide, with distinct mountain chains, and with broad valleys, such as the Copper River, intervening. This mountain system after following the coast almost due north to Cape Spencer turns with the coast line of Alaska to follow the Aleutian Islands, which are really a collection of mountain peaks partially submerged. The Pacific mountain system includes some of the highest peaks in the world, such as Mount McKinley, Mount Wrangell, Mount Logan and Mount St. Elias. Beyond this system is the central plateau which in the states is known as the Inland

Empire. In Alaska this plateau includes that area drained by the Yukon, Kuskokwim and other rivers, and is a gently rolling upland, ranging in altitude from 2,000 to 5,000 feet. Beyond this again is the Rocky Mountain system, called the Endicott Range here, which does not have as high peaks as in the United States. Finally, the Arctic slope, drained chiefly by the Colville River, is merely a continuation of the Great Plains region. This area is not yet fully explored but is known to be rich in minerals.

The mountain system along the coast gives southeastern and southwestern Alaska numerous harbors and steep banked islands. The islands are almost innumerable, and for the most part, particularly in the Aleutian group, are very small, the largest being the islands of Kodiak in western Alaska and Prince of Wales in the southeastern section, both over 100 miles long and averaging about 40 miles in width. The area abounds in fiords, of which the largest are Glacier Bay, Lynn and Portland Canals.

Southeastern Alaska, because of the nature of the coast line, is one of the scenic wonders of the world, and a favorite resort of tourists. Numerous books have been written attempting to describe in unmeasured terms the beauties of the "Inland Passage," by which is meant the steamer trip from Seattle, Washington, to Skagway, a distance of 1,100 miles practically entirely in inland waters with a channel at times so narrow that an ocean-going steamer has barely enough room to go through.

The mountains line the shore of the mainland throughout this area and the route of the steamships follows channels such as Chatham Strait, cutting in between the islands, ranging from a few hundred yards to five or six miles broad and of great depth. In most places the steamer can travel within a few yards of the shore line in perfect safety. The picturesqueness is further enhanced by the thickly timbered hillsides and the numerous streams and fiords extending on both sides of the passage followed by the vessel. Until the establishment of proper safeguards in recent years these narrow passages, so beautiful in summer, were perilous in wintry fogs and snowstorms and brought many a ship to grief. Throughout the northern part of this area are numerous glaciers well known to American visitors, and in their mute way responsible for making Alaska synonymous with the Land of Glaciers, though in fact the glacial area of Alaska is confined to this region and ceases to exist after one reaches the main part of Alaska in the Cook Inlet and Bering Sea areas.

At the northern end of this waterway is Glacier Bay, fittingly named because a half dozen mammoth ice fields hourly deposit icebergs into the waters of the harbor. The northwestern glaciers of this bay—namely, Great Pacific, Rendu and Carroll—are all active; that is, they are moving down their valleys and dropping huge islands of ice into the sea with an almost continuous roar. The rate of the more active has been estimated at about sixteen miles recession in the last six hundred years. This recession has given Canada a harbor at this point, which may or may not remain, depending on future glacial action. The boundary line comes in very close, approximately to the head of these glaciers. The

Childs Glacier near Cordova.

chief drawback to this prospective harbor is that the country inland at this point is very mountainous.

Leaving the southeastern or Alexander Archipelago, the coast line is barren and foreboding, affording practically no protected harbor for several hundred miles. Yakutat Bay is a small anchorage used chiefly by fishing vessels. Controller Bay, at the mouth of Copper River, is also small and unsatisfactory for large ocean-going craft. Near this bay is Kayak Island where Vitus Bering, the discoverer, first landed. Prince William Sound, the first harbor going westward from southeastern Alaska, is destined to be a great center of future Alaska, with its majestic harbor of Resurrection Bay landlocked by large islands. The Sound itself, bordered by mountains rising 6,000 to 7,000 feet is a true fairyland of Alpine beauty. In the hinterland of this Sound is the most mountainous region of Alaska. The coast line bends southward again into Kenai Peninsula, dividing Prince William Sound from Cook Inlet, the largest bay on the Pacific Coast, and containing the most northern ice-free port. The Inlet runs up almost 200 miles to the point where the government railroad last leaves the coast line. From this inlet the Alaska Peninsula, even now only partially explored, extends out into the Aleutian Islands 1,200 miles long and ranges from 20 to 50 miles in width; many of the islands being merely barren rocks and others, such as Unimak, very fertile spots. All the islands abound in volcanic activity.

Beyond the Aleutian Islands the whole geographic aspect changes. The shore line becomes rocky and shallow, with few harbors and no coastal mountains or glaciers. This coastal condition continues throughout the rest of the coast line of Alaska into the Arctic Ocean. From Bristol Bay up to Seward Peninsula the coast is lined with barrier beaches which make small lagoons and of which the most famous is probably Nome Beach, the scene of the Alaskan gold rush of 1899. Inland from these beaches for a distance varying from a few to several miles is the so-called Tundra—a somewhat swampy, peaty lowland cut by numerous streams and supporting little vegetation except moss, flowers and scrub willows.

At Seward Peninsula the coast line juts out to come to its closest proximity with Asia. The sixty-mile breadth of Bering Strait at this point is further lessened by the Diomede Islands in the center of the Strait, so that engineering theorists have dreamt of tunnels or bridges from Alaska to Siberia to make feasible railway traffic between the United States and Europe and Asia. Such a project would face the necessity of at least one span of twenty miles under or over water. The Strait is very shoal, averaging about 150 feet in depth. This creates a strong tide that keeps it free from solid ice almost the year around but there is a tremendous flow of ice through the Strait in the spring and summer months. The mountains already referred to, which line the mainland coast, make up the coast range from the United States to Skagway, ranging from 5,000 to 6,000 feet in height, about 100 miles wide and drained chiefly by the Taku, Stikine and Unuk Rivers. The Stikine near the town of Wrangell and the Chilkat near Skagway afford the two best passes through these mountains to the interior and each was the route of thousands of stampeders in the gold rush of 1898. These mountains are heavily forested on the coast and have a heavy precipitation of snow on the uplands and rain on the coast. North of these is St. Elias range, containing peaks such as Mount Logan, close to 20,000 feet in height, and broken by the Copper River and Thompson Pass, with very little vegetation on the mountains because of their ruggedness. The Aleutian Range, making up the islands, is largely volcanic. The Alaska Range, the northern limit of the Pacific mountain system, averages around 10,000 feet altitude and contains Mount McKinley, reaching up to over 20,000 feet.

Beyond this mountain system is the central plateau, corresponding to the Colorado and Columbia plateaus of the western United States. It is roughly 200 miles wide with deep drainage sometimes 1,000 to 4,000 feet deep, and is roughly the area drained by the Yukon and Kuskokwim Rivers. It is a rolling upland with stunted trees and a continental climate. The altitude ranges from 2,000 to 4,000 feet but at the great bend of the Yukon River the plateau is as low as 500 feet above sea level. The plateau shelves down into the two great deltas of the Yukon and Kuskokwim, covering 25,000 square miles and ranging from an altitude of 100 feet down to sea level. North of the central plateau is the extension of the Rocky Mountain system of the United States, known in Alaska as the Endicott Range, dividing the plateau from the Arctic slope. This range is in reality an echelon of mountain ranges rising as high as 10,000 feet, much of which is still unexplored.

The Arctic slope itself begins in a plateau about 100 miles wide and thence shelves down in tundra to the Arctic Ocean.

The drainage of Alaska is prolific in all districts. The Pacific Coast line is cut by myriads of rapidly flowing streams. In the interior of Alaska there are close to six thousand miles of rivers navigable to steamers. These numerous rivers serve as highways in summer by boat and in winter by sled, as sources of placer mining, water power, timber and arable lands. In the southeastern portion, the Stikine, Taku and Chilkat Rivers are best known. The first mentioned is navigable for about 150 miles, has an average current of five miles per hour, and was the scene of the first gold excitement in 1870 when the Cassiar strike was made. It was also one of the routes to Dawson in '98, as its head waters are in close proximity to the head waters of rivers flowing into Bering Sea and the Arctic Ocean. The other two rivers are not navigable for large boats but have served as passes through the mountains. The Chilkat at the northern end of the inland passage from Seattle is the site of the famous Chilkoot Pass through which thousands of miners found their way to the Klondike, and which now serves in part for the right of way of the White Pass Railway from Skagway to the head waters of the Yukon in Canada. In southwestern Alaska, the Copper River is navigable for small boats and leads to Thompson Pass, the former main route to the central plateau from Valdez on the coast to Fairbanks on the Tanana River. This river is also the route for a railway, tapping perhaps the largest copper mineral section in the world. The Sushitna emptying into Cook Inlet drains an area of 8,000 square miles, mostly very rich land, and serves as a route for the present government railroad.

The central plateau of Alaska drains entirely into the Bering Sea although the source of some of the rivers, particularly the head waters of the Yukon, lies within a few miles of the Pacific Ocean near Skagway. Bristol Bay is fed by two great lakes—Illiamna and Clark—each over fifty miles long and eight to ten miles wide—and by a series of close to 500 other lakes, discovered within the last few years, which makes this area a veritable "Baby Mediterranean." North of Bristol Bay is the Kuskokwim system, draining an area of over 50,000 square miles, and navigable 500 miles to the town of McGrath and debouching into a delta of twenty or thirty miles. In many places it lies close to the Yukon, but much of the district is as yet unexplored. The largest river in Alaska is the Yukon—2,300 miles long and draining 330,000 square miles, about half of which is in Alaska. It is the fifth largest river in North America, comparing in size with the St. Lawrence. Steamers navigate the river for over 2,000 miles or throughout its Alaskan course during the open season from June to September. Some idea of its size will be gained from observations made at the boundary line 1,800 miles from the mouth. At this point it is 1,300 feet wide, averaging 2,000 feet in these upper reaches, the channel itself being about 600 feet wide and over 20 feet deep, with an average current of three to five miles per hour. The river looms large in the life of interior

Alaska. The mark of the pioneer or "Sourdough" is that he has seen the ice come and go in the Yukon. After the original gold strike in the Canadian Klondike, the horde of gold seekers spread into Alaska down the Yukon and its tributaries developing new fields all the way.

Among its tributaries probably the most famous is the Klondike—a small river, all in Canada, flowing in a high plateau region with numerous deep and wide branching valleys, sometimes rising to 1,500 feet above the water. The many small streams cutting through this plateau into the Klondike were the scene in 1898 of one of the greatest excitements that has gripped the world in modern times. The Tanana River traversed by steamers for 200 miles drains an area of 25,000 square miles which conservatively can furnish enough food for a future population of Alaska many times the present size. The Koyukuk, navigable for 600 miles, drains an equal area and stretches into the Arctic Circle. All of these rivers are characterized by relatively strong currents, great erosion which has made possible the placer gold deposits through the district, and shifting channels that are the bane of river pilots.

Climate

Enough has been said already to show that there is more misinformation about Alaska than about almost any other equal territory in the world, but in considering the climate of this country more entrenched false notions must be discarded than in any other subject. At the outset we should disabuse our minds of the idea that the farther north we go the colder it becomes. Three equal factors determine temperature—the distance north from the equator, the height above the sea and the distance from the sea. In Alaska, there are few localities where all three factors combine equally. In the first place, it is wrong to speak of the "climate of Alaska," the proper term being "climates," as the country has at least eight climatic provinces, each distinct in its way. Ever since some misguided and certainly misinformed publicist characterized Seward's purchase of Alaska as an "ice-box," the country has labored under the great handicap of firmly entrenched general ignorance as to its true climate. This tendency of the people of the United States to look upon Alaska as a land of ice and snow has been aided materially by the proneness of writers, both fiction and otherwise, to describe Alaska as ice-bound, and the home of fur-clad, tallow-eating people. The poems of Service and the books of Jack London, though admirable in many ways, have been leaders in this false gospel, as their scenes are laid near the Arctic Circle. The chief Russian industry in Alaska was the trapping of furs with which we associate arctic conditions. Tourists visiting Alaska comment only on features to which they are unaccustomed, such as icebergs and northern conditions. Moreover, the greatest contact that our countrymen have had with Alaska was through the gold rush, which centered about the coldest regions of the country. Even government employees have helped this general impression by giving their books or articles such titles as "Our Arctic Province."

As a matter of fact, the southeastern and southwestern

parts of Alaska within one hundred miles of the coast, and the whole Aleutian Peninsula, have a climate more equable than that of New England. Practically all the harbors of Alaska opening on the Pacific Ocean are free of ice throughout the year. Even the Arctic Circle regions, which may be called an Arctic province, have not the severe climate ordinarily associated with such a term. The average temperature there approximates fairly closely that of the northwestern United States, such as Montana, Minnesota and the Dakotas. People live there comfortably in winter, their chief inconvenience being blizzards. In summer, temperatures as high as 100 degrees have been reported. As Stefansson points out, scientifically the polar regions in midsummer have more heat per square mile than the equator. Fort McPherson, 65 miles within the Arctic Circle, recorded an average temperature for its warmest month of 58 degrees, only one degree less than that of San Francisco. The chief climatic disadvantage in Alaska is the unequal distribution of sunlight, yet the peoples of the Scandinavian countries seem to thrive and increase under similar conditions.

The great controlling element in Alaska's climate is "Kuro Siwo" or "black stream," which is the term applied to the Japanese current because of the deep blue waters. This current, rising in the equatorial regions of the Pacific Ocean, is larger than the Gulf Stream of the Eastern United States. It washes the coasts of southeastern and southwestern Alaska with an average temperature of about 50 degrees, which is carried on to the shores by prevailing westerly winds.

In southeastern Alaska zero weather in winter is a rarity. Skating and coasting are winter sports that can be enjoyed for only a few days during the entire winter. The average summer temperature is well over 50 degrees and the average winter temperature around 30 degrees. It has an ideal climate, comparing favorably with that of Washington, D. C., except for the heavy rainfall. Sitka, the former capital, shows one record for a year of 105 inches of rainfall. Unalaska in the Aleutian Islands is even worse in this respect, having recorded one year with only eight clear days. The snowfall of countries in a similar latitude here turns to rain or fog, making such conditions common in all seasons except summer. At Valdez, on Prince William Sound, the temperature range is about 10 degrees lower than that of southeastern Alaska, and this is the area of the greatest snowfall in the country, with a fall of often seven to eight feet. The climate of Cook Inlet and southwestern Alaska is probably the best in Alaska as it is not too severe and has just enough rain for an ideal climate.

Probably the best way to form an accurate idea of the climate is to note the mean temperatures compiled over the period since Alaska became a part of the United States. Fort Tongass on the southern boundary has a mean annual temperature of 47.8 degrees; Sitka, 43.3 degrees; the Island of Kodiak, 40.6 degrees. Compare these with Scotland, 46.1 degrees; Ottawa, Canada, 42.1 degrees; Christiania, Norway, 41.9 degrees and Finland, 39.2 degrees. In forty years Point Barrow, the most northern town in Alaska, never recorded a temperature lower than 54 degrees below zero and Nome no lower than 45 degrees below. Towns in Montana have recorded 68 degrees below, in New England 45 degrees, in New York 46 degrees and in North Dakota 54 degrees. The range of temperature in southeastern Alaska is very slight, that at Sitka being only 26 degrees, whereas in the Yukon Valley the range is 77 degrees. The warmest month in the Yukon Valley has practically the same temperature as the warmest month in southeastern Alaska. This, coupled with the long periods of daylight in summer, makes agriculture a practicable future resource of the Yukon Valley.

The North has held terrors for the average man from the earliest historic days, probably because our first ancestors came from southern climes. Down through the ages, the horrors of cold and darkness have persisted, whether they referred to the unknown north of Tacitus, which to him was modern Germany, or whether they refer to the Lenin Land, skirting the North Pole of to-day. The ideas that we ordinarily associate with missionaries suffering hardships and of Arctic explorers overcoming tremendous handicaps are difficult to correct, so much so that explorers carrying on their work in temperatures in which school children attend classes in Minnesota and Manitoba are esteemed heroes. Even the song which most nearly approaches the national anthem for Alaska, entitled "Alaska, my Alaska," is full of such phrases as "Oh, land of ice and snow."

It will be a long, slow process of education that will convince the thoughtful reader that the Arctic is not always cold, is not devoid of vegetation but prolific in it, is not devoid of animal life even in the depth of winter, and is not overpowering either in its deathly stillness, which never exists, or in its gloomy darkness, which has been grossly exaggerated. Modern science tells us that there is no place on the world's surface where there would be in summer forty continuous days of daylight and in winter forty continuous days of darkness. The sun at the North Pole is probably visible seven and one-half months of the year and invisible four and one-half months, but the absence of sun does not mean darkness any more than the absence of direct sunlight inside of a building means darkness at high noon in civilized countries. These new gospels have been the labors of such explorers as Stefansson, and our other modern honest investigators of the Arctic waste. Their refutations in regard to Arctic conditions should become overpowering when applied to those portions of Alaska lying south of the Arctic circle.

RESOURCES

In this tremendous territory with its varied geographical features, Alaska has untold resources which have already produced close to a billion dollars and whose total future output no one would be rash enough to predict. President Harding, after his tour of the country, was most impressed with the resources and devoted his last public utterance before his death to a plea for the preservation of them. The problem confronting this government to-day is the proper use of these resources rather than the two extremes which have been all too well known to Alaskans in the past—namely, misuse or air-tight conservation. Minerals and furs are the first two things that the lay person thinks of when Alaskan resources are mentioned. These are certainly major products but are far from being the chief exports of the territory to-day.

Geologists rate Alaska as having the greatest variety of minerals in the world. Comparatively it is said to have more gold than California and Colorado, more copper than Montana and Arizona and more coal than Pennsylvania, West Virginia and Ohio. Southeastern Alaska has already produced gold and copper in great quantities and will continue to do so indefinitely. The geologic character of the Alexander Archipelago, as this section is known, makes mining in some ways uncertain, inasmuch as a promising vein may peter away to nothing to reopen again in another fissure. Nevertheless, extensive operations have been carried on there, and with the advent of capital even more extensive development will be undertaken.

The Bering River section, lying northwest of southeastern Alaska and within 100 miles of Cordova, is one of the great coal and oil regions of Alaska. Farther to the westward, the government railroad taps two very large coal sections—Matanuska, 200 miles from the ocean terminus, and Healey, or Nenana, in the interior. Gold is also found here in paying quantities. Cordova and the Copper River section are the locale of the Kennecott Mine, for many years the world's richest copper mine. On the Alaska Peninsula coal and oil have been discovered in the Cold Bay region adjacent to Kodiak Island, and this promises to be a center of the future oil industry.

Stand of Spruce in Alaska Tongass forest.

The Kuskokwim River basin is Alaska's most unknown country even to-day, but quicksilver and gold are known deposits there. On the Seward Peninsula gold, silver and tin are being mined in great paying quantities. Cape Lisburne, Point Barrow and the whole Arctic slope is more or less unexplored, but has been definitely proved to be a source of great coal and oil deposits. In the interior, the upper Yukon River, though one of the earliest sections to be prospected, has only been touched, so far as mineral resources are concerned.

Timber is confined principally to the Tongass and Chugach forest reservations. These reservations contain great areas of forests; Tongass forest in southeastern Alaska being close to 30,000 square miles. It is estimated that Sitka spruce and Alpine hemlock comprise 70% of the total growth of timber in Alaska. This timber is not of superior quality or as fit for lumber as the fir and spruce forests of the Pacific Northwest of the United States. The distant market adds to the difficulties of developing a lumbering industry in Alaska though close to 20 million board feet are cut there now annually. There is, however, an excellent possibility for a pulp industry, and southeastern Alaskan forests alone are probably of sufficient extent to provide a permanent pulp industry equal to one-third of the present total consumption of pulp in the United States. This industry would be helped by the heavy rainfall, in that the forests have rapid growth and are fairly free from the great natural dangers of fire or insects. The Yukon Valley is studded with islands of forests, for the most part made up of stunted willow growth. The

Seward Peninsula has a considerable forest area but the bulk of Alaska's forests are in the two reservations previously named.

The fisheries of Alaska rank with minerals as the greatest product to-day. Salmon have abounded in the numerous coastal streams of the territory; cod, halibut, eulachon, herring, shrimp and many other species of fish are caught in commercial quantities, particularly in the Gulf of Alaska and the streams emptying into it. The whaling industry was one of the greatest of Alaska's industries in the middle of the last century but has been almost exhausted, and is not of as great value since the advent of Rockefeller and Standard Oil.

Furs were the chief attraction to the Russians throughout their tenure of this territory but, as in other parts of the world, the advent of civilization has checked this industry, although it will continue to be a very large one indefinitely. Its permanence will be helped by the rapid growth of fur farming, particularly fox farming on the many islands of the coast. The greatest fur in historical importance is that of the seal, whose home is on the Pribilof Islands in Bering Sea. Under governmental control the seal herd is increasing, and its permanence as a commercial product is guaranteed. The other fur-bearing animals of Alaska include mink, marten, otter, bear and almost every specie of value to-day. The animals originally were found in all sections, now they exist only in the wilder parts of the interior.

One of the newest resources of Alaska, and a transplanted one, is that of the reindeer. An importation of 1,000 reindeer from Lapland has grown in thirty years to almost 400,000, divided into over 100 herds. The reindeer was imported primarily as a source of food for the Esquimaux but has increased so rapidly that it bids fair to become an article of food in all parts of the world.

Agriculture has been the last of the resources of Alaska to be tapped but already government experimental stations there have proved beyond doubt that the country can support in foodstuffs whatever population may be attracted to it. There are millions of acres of arable land in the valleys of the great rivers. The growing season in southeastern Alaska is approximately 200 days a year, in Cook Inlet 100 days and in the interior from 50 to 100 days. All these advantages, combined with the long period of intensive sunlight through an exceptionally clear atmosphere due to the lack of dust show that the country will surpass its Scandinavian counterpart in agricultural resources.

Alaska is in the same latitude as Norway, Sweden and Finland and has a larger arable area than all three combined. These countries now support populations running into millions, so that some idea of the quantity of Alaska's future agricultural output can be formed.

CHAPTER II

ETHNOLOGY

THE aboriginal inhabitants of Alaska may be divided into four great groups—the Esquimaux or Inuit, the Aleut, the Athapascan and the Thlingit. There are two minor races occupying small areas in southeastern Alaska—the Haida and Tsimpshian. The Esquimaux inhabits the coast of Alaska roughly from the Alaska Peninsula north and throughout the Arctic region. The Aleuts are a branch of the Esquimaux but they had a distinctive development due to their isolated location on the Aleutian Islands. The Thlingit occupy southeastern Alaska and parts of southwestern Alaska along the coast. The Athapascan is one of the largest linguistic families of North America. The Alaskan branches of it occupy the interior of the country. The Haida are located on Prince of Wales Island in southeastern Alaska and the Tsimpshian are a colony on Annette Island. The last two are offshoots of their tribes which are settled in British Columbia.

The Esquimaux or, as he calls himself, the Inuit, meaning people, is very much like the other Esquimaux of the Arctic except that the Alaskan branch has been contaminated by the civilization of the white man to a greater extent. Their origin is still in doubt. The weight of scientific research seems to agree that they originated somewhere in the middle of the North American continent, possibly around the Peace River or Great Slave Lake region of Canada from whence they migrated north and west. Against this there are many plausible theories that they originated in Asia and came over Bering Strait or with the drift of the Japan current, some authorities even going so far as to place their origin in France. The coastal tribes on both sides of Bering Sea have probably moved back and forth between Asia and America. They are of medium stature, of great strength and endurance. They have small hands and feet, Mongol eyes and broad faces. They are considered of peaceable nature, cheerful, truthful, honest but very immoral. The popular notion that they live on oil or blubber has been exploded completely—they are meat-eaters largely. Their lives are very transitory, their chief occupation being the chase. They formerly hunted the caribou in summer and the seal and other sea mammals in winter. In summer they live in skin tents which in winter are covered with snow or discarded for snow houses, and resemble turkish baths at all seasons. They are very intelligent, good draughtsmen and carvers, and lovers of poetry and music. Their village life is loose, under a chief who has very little power. Their habits, their belief in Shamanism and Tabu have been dilated upon at length by Arctic explorers so that no extensive treatment of them here is necessary. Along with the other native races they have decreased rapidly because of their contact with civilization, and eventually they may be exterminated.

The importation of reindeer which has grown tremendously has checked starvation among the more southern villages, but the northern Esquimaux is primarily a hunter and does not take readily to the settled life of a herder. The whaling industry which reached its height in these regions in the decade from 1880 to 1890 brought with it mostly evils to these easily influenced aborigines. Firearms have reaped havoc with their scanty supply of wild life. Outwardly their culture is that of the white man. The fairly dense inland population of primitive days has disappeared, and these inland Esquimaux have gone to the coast, as the coast natives were the first to be wiped out by the softening influence of civilization and by the ravages of contagious diseases, chiefly tuberculosis, measles, smallpox and venereal diseases. More recently they have shown a tendency to adapt themselves to their new conditions and should continue to maintain a small nucleus in this far northern region where the white man will penetrate slowly.

The Aleuts are a branch of the Esquimaux and receive their distinctive name from the early Russians—the name being the Indian word for islands. They are probably more intelligent than the Esquimaux but less independent. The early history of Russian occupation is one long tale of shameful treatment by the uncouth traders and explorers. Originally the Aleuts numbered close to 30,000 but their mistreatment reduced their number to about 2,000, most of whom were enslaved. Bishop Veniaminoff brought with him a new attitude on the part of Russia toward these children, and since his advent in about 1820 the race has fared better but has not prospered. To-day such a large proportion have intermarried with the Russians that they may almost be classed as an extinct race.

The interior natives were never very numerous and as a whole have a history of extreme hostility to the white man. They are divided into three tribes. The Kutchin on the Porcupine and Tanana Rivers were extremely warlike and decimated their own numbers by the evil practice of killing their female children. The Ahtena, or ice people, were found in the region of Copper River. They were especially hostile and murderous to early explorers. They were people of good physique and were a hunting and fishing race. They preserved themselves by acting as middlemen between the coast tribes and the interior. The Ahtena probably number now less than 100 adults in all. The Khotana, living on the lower Yukon and Cook Inlet, retain early adopted Esquimaux traits and have practically merged with the Inuit.

The Thlingits of southeastern Alaska are a part of the Koluschan linguistic family originating in British Columbia and now found from the southern boundary of Alaska to Controller Bay. They were very warlike and drove out the first Russian settlement at Sitka in 1802 when Baranof tried to import Aleuts to that district. They are mostly a fisher folk, and able to wrest a fairly easy sustenance from the numerous waters of the Archipelago. This life made them very good canoe builders as the dug-out was indispensable to their existence. They are also excellent carvers and weavers of baskets and blankets. There are two great clans—the Raven and the Wolf. For years the Thlingit population showed a steady decline from the earliest authentic figure of close to 10,000. In early days they had an extensive social organization and practiced slave holding so much that one census lists 900 slaves, and Chief Shakes at

Wrangell has been said to have had 100 slaves in his retinue when the first white man came to his district. The "Potlatch" was one of their great feasts, when the prominent Indian gained social prestige and influence by the open-handedness with which he gave gifts to his visitors. One Potlatch on record lasted five days, during which a family gave away 500 blankets, 50 rifles, 300 steel traps and tons of food, which had been accumulating for more than fifteen years.

Their totems, which record the family life in carved cedar trees rising sometimes to the height of fifty feet, carry the tribal emblem and are the coat of arms or crests of the Indian families. These record the history, genealogy, legend or memorial of some great event, and serve as a publication to the world of the status of the owner. Their canoes, carved from great cedar trees, were seaworthy enough to carry parties of twenty or thirty to all parts of southeastern Alaska and even a thousand miles south to the present United States.

The Chilkat Indians in the vicinity of Skagway, noted for their blanket and basket work, were not given to wars among themselves save as retribution for an unprovoked murder, such as the Sitka-Wrangell feud which was not settled until the coming of the whites. One of the last Thlingit chieftians to survive was Chief Shakes at Wrangell. He was as proud as any noble of our race and lived in memories of a glorious past. It is a sad commentary on our civilization that his death was caused by an accident while intoxicated and his son was murdered in a drunken brawl.

The Haidas are centered about Queen Charlotte Sound in

Thlingit dug-out canoe, Wrangell.

British Columbia. The Alaskan branch, known as the Kaigani, drove out the Thlingits from the south end of Prince of Wales Island about 200 years ago and have several villages there to-day. They proved their adaptability to the secular side of civilization but have never taken kindly to the teachings of the missionary. They are probably the best carvers and painters and are above the average intellectually. This hardy race has been reduced to one-tenth of its former strength in the last 60 years.

The Tsimpshian is a small race with a language peculiar to itself. They were probably an inland people and now inhabit the Skeena and Nass Rivers of British Columbia. In 1891 Father Duncan of the Episcopal church transferred a colony of close to a thousand to Annette Island, where they are now maintained on a government reservation.

Trade between the natives and whites was carried on by means of trade jargons, such as the Chinook Jargon known to thousands of pioneers to-day. Such a makeshift, part English, part French, and part Indian, was necessary as these primitive peoples have languages which are far from simple. Stefansson estimates that it is as difficult to master Esquimaux as it is to learn four European languages. Our respect for their intelligence mounts when we consider that the average Esquimaux commands a vocabulary of about ten thousand words, comparable to that of a college graduate of our highly cultured race, whereas the average American citizen commands a vocabulary of about 2,000 words.

Some idea of the manner in which civilization has broken down these southeastern Indians may be gained from the effect that salmon canneries have had on them. In the old days each family owned a creek where the members would put out their small nets and catch enough fish which by drying and smoking would tide them over the winter months. Now the canneries place traps as large as our metropolitan wharves far out at sea where the salmon are caught almost before they enter the inland waterways. The Indian is forced to work in the cannery and these improvident people have difficulty in saving enough money from the uncertain cannery season to tide them over the winter. Formerly, the Indians hardened their children by throwing them into the ocean each morning. They dressed in furs or blankets and lived an outdoor life; their houses were loosely built and well ventilated. Now, they are taking to tight houses and stoves that eat up the air, and the white man's clothing and mode of life. This makes them easy prey to tuberculosis and other diseases, while the white man, borrowing a leaf from their book, has moved his tubercular cases back to tents. However, the period of adaptation to new modes of life has been accomplished and the present generation seems to be sturdy. They are becoming more independent and self-supporting; and the government has given them an opportunity to become citizens, after following, for fifty years, the blind policy of neither making them wards on a reservation or allowing them to become citizens.

The missionary in Alaska, as elsewhere, was the sole saving grace of civilization when the roughest side of our life, the pioneer element, was first presented to the Indians. An outstanding example of the missionary spirit is that already referred to of William Duncan, the young English missionary who came alone to the Tsimpshians of British Columbia when they were in a state bordering on cannibalism. He took a thousand of his wards to Annette Island where he established the town of Metlakatla. This town is now run entirely by natives and includes a saw mill and cannery, both successfully managed by them. Their church is one of the largest in Alaska. Duncan built well so that his work has persisted after his death. He well merits the title of "Apostle of Alaska." Similar attempts at transplanting these Indians, as in the coöperative enterprise at Saxman near Ketchikan, were not nearly so successful.

The Russian missionary work started with Bishop Innocent Veniaminoff, whose sway in Alaska between 1820 and 1840 was the most beneficent of any of the Greek churchmen. Father Herman and Father Juvenal have been called "Alaska's Saints" for the great work that they did among the Aleuts and southwestern Indians. The Greek church still maintains its influence in the Aleutian Islands and has a church at Sitka, which is one of the show places of this country.

The Presbyterians went into Alaska at about the time of the purchase, and have been probably the most zealous workers of the Protestant faith. Their zeal gave them great power at Washington and this reacted inevitably to Alaska's detriment as their advice was often bigoted or narrow. Sheldon Jackson and S. Hall Young are two men whose names are intimately connected with the early history of Alaska, Jackson being the one who was chiefly instrumental in introducing the reindeer. Anglicanism came into Alaska from the interior with the Hudson Bay Company as early as 1851. Their great leader is Bishop P. T. Rowe, one of the great churchmen of the country. The Roman Catholics have been leaders in this country as they were in Canada. The Jesuits established their mission at Holy Cross on the Yukon River very early in the history of American occupation. Archbishop Seghers, their martyr, and Bishop Crimont are the leaders they point to with pride.

By and large the work of the missionaries was very slow to bear fruit. The Esquimaux was loath to give up his shaman, and the Thlingit his medicine man. The Indian went to church curiously and stayed to get the trinkets of the missionary. Their tribal superstitions and rites are still observed to this day. The islands of southeastern Alaska are dotted with their graves covered by totems, and in places even substantial houses, testimonials of Indian cults. But certainly the aboriginal Alaskan would have fared far worse had it not been for the work of missionaries.

The 1890 census gave the following numbers to these divisions:

Esquimaux	14,012
Thlingit	4,737
Athapascan	500
Aleut	3,439
Tsimpshian	952
Haida	391

The first accurate census—probably that of 1900—gave the total Indian population as 30,000, including in this number creoles. At the present time they number about 25,000.

There is nothing in this history of local conditions of Alaskan natives to show that their future may be different from that of any other primitive races when a superior race has entered. It is probable that the process of intermarriage with the whites will go on, together with the gradual extermination of isolated villages by such epidemics as influenza and smallpox. To-day the Alaskan aborigine and his totem monuments are attractions for the growing tourist trade to the region. These attractions will continue to be enhanced as they become more rare. Their story is the familiar one of the vanishing race and their contribution to Alaskan history has practically ceased.

CHAPTER III

DISCOVERY AND EXPLORATION

THE geographic position of Alaska has been at once a prime factor in aiding and in deterring its discovery and exploration. Situated as it is on the northwest corner of the Continent of North America, with the forbidding territories of Siberia and northern Canada on either side, and lying far to the north of the regular trade routes of the Pacifiic Ocean, the country would not logically be the subject of investigation or enterprise until Siberia or Canada had been peopled to a point close enough for civilization to hear of it. Once, however, Alaska had been brought to the attention of civilized man, the long coast line, with its excellent harbors and its mild climate, would invite coastal exploration. This would be further aided by the juxtaposition to Asia at Bering Strait, where the two continents are only sixty miles apart, and more especially at the Aleutian Islands, which are practically intervisible one to another.

Alaskan history from its discovery down to fairly recent times does not belong so much to North America as to Asia. This perspective is admirably brought out by Professor F. A. Golder, who regards the discovery of Alaska as a closing incident in the century of Russian expansion eastward in Asia. The North American history of Alaska certainly did not begin until the opening of the nineteenth century when the triangular trade between the northwest coast and China flourished, or even possibly as late as the international disputes with regard to Alaska in the 1820's.

The rapid and at the same time cruel march of the conquering Russians is a necessary prelude to the story of Alaska. The pioneer Russian traders, or promishleniki, have often been cited as forerunners of one of the most rapid colonizing movements in modern history. They crossed the Ural Mountains in the sixteenth century and reached the Amur as early as 1640, where they came in conflict with the Chinese. They had succeeded in crossing the whole of Asia by the middle of the century and were exploring Kamchatka by 1713. Scarcely a generation passed between the arrival on the Pacific Ocean and the discovery of Alaska. Some idea of the rapidity of this movement in Asia may be gained by recalling that while these Russians were pushing their settlements thousands of miles, western Europeans had barely succeeded in going from the Atlantic seaboard of the present United States to the Mississippi River, a distance of a few hundred miles. At the same time, too much credit should not be given these promishleniki. They were pushed forward by the great expansionist movement that gripped all Russia and has made that country the largest land holder in the world to-day. If Deshneff, Gwosdeff or Bering had not succeeded, others would have been successful in the same ventures within a very short time.

These semi-civilized Europeans and Asiatics did not present a beautiful spectacle for history in their march across the Siberian wastes. They conquered the Chukchi Indians either by thoroughly cowing them or killing them with all manner of torture. For the most part the commanding officers were of inferior caliber and mutinies in the ranks were a common occurence. The "Woewod," as the Siberian governor was known, used his term of office to exploit his territory in every conceivable way, and corruption as well as peculation was considered entirely proper. As late as 1720 nothing was known of America north of the present limits of California and nothing of Asia north of Novo Zemlya. With the advent of the Russians on the shores of the Pacific came rumors of a land across the sea known variously as Terra de Jeso, Gama Land, Company Land and State Island. These mythical countries were invested with tales of fabulous wealth like the famous Seven Cities of Coronado. Maps generally after 1650 showed a strait known usually as Anian, from the Chinese province of Marco Polo. The lands to the east of this strait were generally held to be islands, and it was years after Bering's voyage before his discoveries were definitely established as part of North America.

There is one possible exception to this lack of knowledge of Alaska arising from the tale of Simeon Deshneff, who in 1648 claimed to have sailed from the Kolyma, on the Arctic Ocean shores of Siberia, around East Cape to the Anadir River, in Bering Sea. His story has been copied without proof by many writers, beginning with Muller, but is attacked with great weight by Dr. Golder. Certainly if Deshneff performed this feat he was an intrepid navigator and leader, and the greatest honor should be bestowed upon him. However, all evidence seems to be against his claim. Perhaps the greatest evidence is that although many far more able navigators, and far better equipped, attempted the same voyage later, they universally failed, and it was not until the work of Baron Wrangell in 1821, combined with that of Vitus Bering in 1728, Cook in 1778 and Billings in 1787, that Asia and America were conclusively proved to be separate continents.

The earliest references to Alaska are shrouded in uncertainty. The term "Alaska" comes from the native word meaning "great country" and was applied by them to the present Alaska peninsula. Early explorers understood the word to mean an island—probably one of the larger islands in Bering Sea. There is mention of a certain Popoff who in 1711 went to East Cape, the easternmost point of Siberia, and mentions Alaska in his despatches. There is also the story of Michael Gwosdeff, the geodist. He sailed to East Cape in 1732, using one of Bering's ships during the latter's absence. On the voyage, he skirted an unknown land which he refers to as an island in his note, written ten years after the event; this was probably one of the Diomedes. He also speaks of seeing a distant land, which may possibly have been Alaska but very probably could have been another island.

It is the part of pedantry rather than erudition to strive to give credit to Deshneff, Gwosdeff or any of these other doubtful voyagers for the discovery of Alaska. The achievement of such an important task should be credited to the person who can scientifically prove his case. If this be done the name of Vitus Bering and the date 1741 can be accepted as authentic data for the discovery of Alaska. In so doing we take no more credit from these earlier navigators than we do from the Norsemen who possibly or even probably preceded Columbus to the shores of America.

Vitus Bering, of Danish descent, was born in 1681. He was a sailor in the employ of the East India Company before joining the Russian Navy, where he rose rapidly from the ranks. In 1725, he was appointed by Peter the Great as the most capable man to seek a passage to India and China through the Arctic. The great Czar of Russia had dreamed of attaining fame in the arts and sciences for Russia by discovering a northeast passage ever since his early travels in Holland. He was now to issue the orders launching this expedition on the eve of his death. The orders received by Bering, with marginal notes in Peter's own hand were: first, to go to Kamchatka and build two vessels; secondly, to go to the northernmost point of Siberia and discover whether or not Asia joined America; third, to look for settlements on the American coast or the vessel of a western nation; finally, to draw up an account of all of his explorations and return to St. Petersburg. The voyage in all its ramifications lasted until 1749, long after the death of Bering himself.

The orders are significant in listing as the first accomplishment the overland trip to Kamchatka and the building of vessels. This trip was in itself a great undertaking and was carried through successfully by the commander. The building of the vessels on the shores of a primitive country with materials that had to be transported thousands of miles was also accomplished successfully and Bering sailed on his

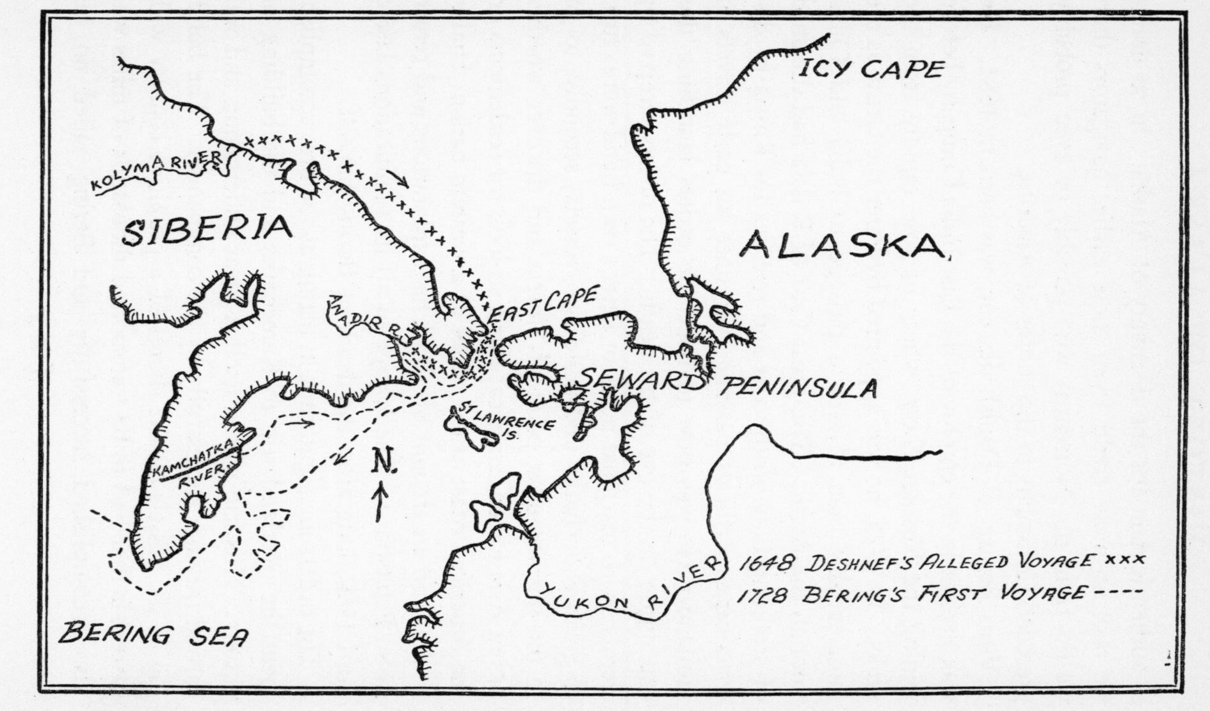
ICY CAPE
KOLYMA RIVER
SIBERIA
ALASKA
ANADIR R.
EAST CAPE
SEWARD PENINSULA
ST LAWRENCE IS.
KAMCHATKA RIVER
N.
YUKON RIVER
1648 DESHNEF'S ALLEGED VOYAGE xxx
1728 BERING'S FIRST VOYAGE ----
BERING SEA

first voyage in 1728. He went up the coast of Asia as far as Icy Cape, where he observed the land turning westward and concluded that he had definitely proved that Asia and America were not united. This proof as we have seen was not finally established for a century. Though he was less than 100 miles from Alaska he did not see its shores because of the foggy weather. Had he stayed long enough to take the scientific observations proper to such a voyage he would no doubt have discovered Alaska then. His apparent failure almost doomed his whole expedition because of official detraction at St. Petersburg. However, the Empress Anne, and after her the Empress Catherine, listened favorably to his personal report made in 1732, which included his opinion that America was 100 to 250 miles from Kamchatka. He was granted permission to continue his explorations. While he was in Russia, Gwosdeff had made his discoveries in Bering's ship, the "St. Gabriel."

Bering was now close to sixty years of age and did not enter into his second voyage with very much enthusiasm. Consequently, preparations lagged and complaints of his inefficiency were numerous. The voyage finally began in the spring of 1741. The expedition included the "St. Peter," on which Bering himself sailed with Steller, the German naturalist, whose account of the voyage is one of our best authorities for the discovery. Lieutenant Chirikoff was in command of the "St. Paul," with De la Croyere as scientific observer. The two ships kept together until June 20th when, partially due to stormy weather and partially to ill feeling between the chief and his aide, they were separated off the

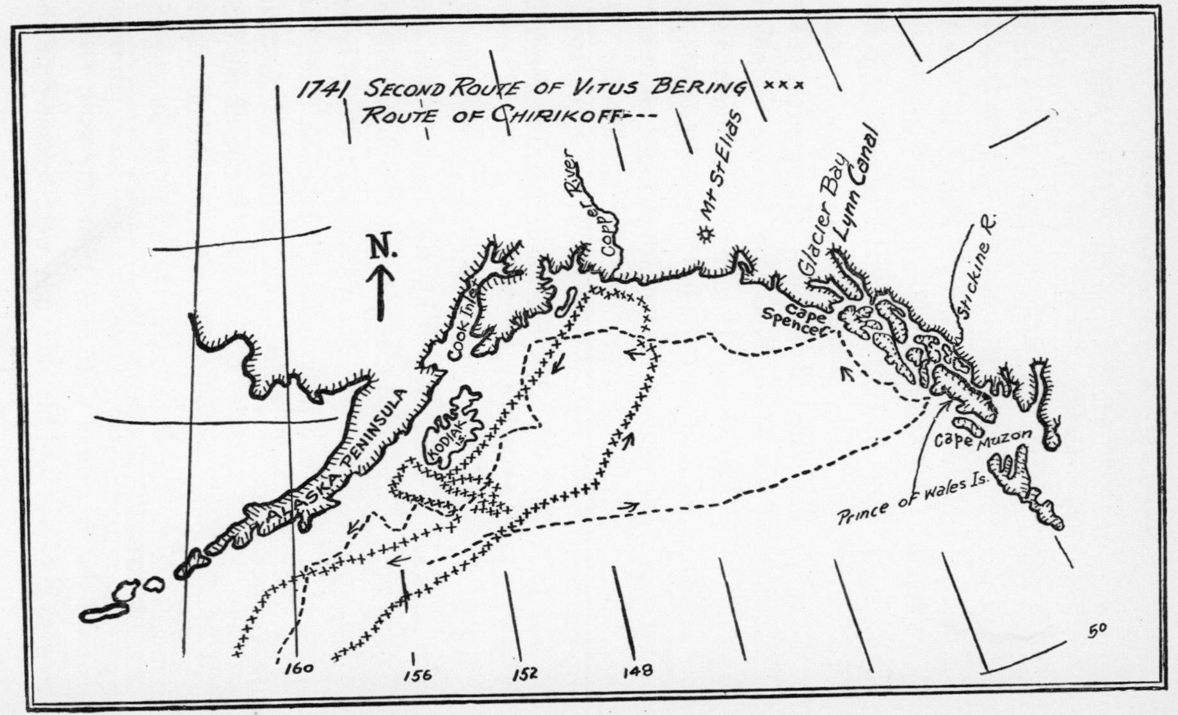
1741 SECOND ROUTE OF VITUS BERING ×××
ROUTE OF CHIRIKOFF---
N.
Cook Inlet
Copper River
Mt St Elias
Glacier Bay
Lynn Canal
Stickine R.
Cape Spencer
Cape Muzon
Prince of Wales Is.
KODIAK Is.
ALASKA PENINSULA
160
156
152
148
50

coast of the Aleutian Islands. After sailing vainly about for several days searching for one another they resumed their voyage, Chirikoff sailing almost due east, and Bering slightly north of due east. The "St. Paul" continued until on July 15, 1741, Chirikoff discovered the coast of Alaska just north of Cape Muzon, the present southern boundary. His chief had changed his course to due north, and first saw Alaska at Mt. St. Elias on July 16th.

Chirikoff after skirting the shores of southeastern Alaska sent a small party ashore near the present site of Sitka to secure water. This party failed to return and a second party also disappeared. When hostile natives approached his vessel, Chirikoff decided to set sail and retraced his way to Siberia after much suffering. Bering landed a small party on an island near Prince William Sound to secure provisions and water. Despite the elation of the party the commander was discouraged even when he made his great discovery. Scurvy was ravaging the man already weighed down by his sixty years, and his anxiety to get back home overcame the zeal of Steller who was in the midst of collecting valuable data for his study of the virgin wild life of the country. The "St. Peter" followed the Alaska Peninsula and Aleutian Islands until driven south by storms to the Commander Islands where the vessel was wrecked on Bering Island. Here the commander sickened and died. His men managed to gather $100,000 worth of furs and constructed a boat from the wreckage of the "St. Peter" and finally regained Siberia. Bering's work cannot be praised too highly for its daring and perseverance. For eight years he struggled against tremendous difficulties with wretched materials, poor tools, and with men continually suffering from scurvy. His vessels were of the rudest sort built of logs covered by rough hewn planks held to the ribs by thongs in lieu of nails and caulked with moss. With such means he discovered a great territory whose value in 1926 compares favorably with that of North America in 1741, and in 2126 it may compare just as favorably with the North America of to-day. His discoveries pushed the dominions of the Czars to their greatest extent. With the exploitation and colonization that Russian America was to see in the next century he settled the geographic problems of northeastern Asia and northwestern America.

While giving due credit to Vitus Bering and his crew we must not stress the ability of the man too greatly. He lacked the vision or single-handed and single-minded purpose of Columbus. He did not conceive the project nor was he responsible for its initiation. He was essentially a plodder, oftentimes lacking the enthusiasm of his followers, and cannot be said to have done more than carry out the task set for him by such dreamers and empire builders as Peter the Great. Yet a comparison of the accomplishments of Bering with Columbus, without any idea of elevating Bering to the same historical significance, would be interesting. Columbus sailed seventy days from Spain before he discovered America, but only 36 days after leaving the last traces of civilization. Bering was cut off from civilization for 54 days of sailing before he discovered Alaska. Columbus was probably about 46 years old when he sailed, Bering was 60;

Columbus had a fleet of three ships with 90 men on each; Bering had two vessels with 76 men on each; Columbus' flag ship, the "Santa Maria," measured approximately 90′ long by 20′ beam and his other two vessels were considerably smaller; Bering's two ships were each 80′ long by 20′ beam. The immediate profits from Columbus' voyage were nil in that he returned with a very meager quantity of gold and a few Indian captives, but his discovery opened limitless possibilities and a new world. The immediate profits of Bering's voyage were $100,000 in furs, and this cargo awakened the lust of a horde of adventurers who within a few years started exploiting Alaska. The eventual possibilities opened by the voyage are limited but they are far greater than any dreamed of in the eighteenth century.

Russia's claims to this great territory were based chiefly on the work of Bering and his lieutenant, because other nations were to outstrip her in the exploration of Alaska. The Russian traders were quick to respond to the story of Bering's discovery and they soon descended upon the Aleutian Islands to exploit them of their furs. Official Russia, however, was practically inactive for twenty-five years; no Russian reached the mainland of Alaska again until 1761. The real Russian exploration of Alaska was not undertaken until practically the opening of the nineteenth century.

Geography affected the exploration of Alaska as profoundly as its discovery. The proximity of the coast line to Asia and its accessibility invited early coastal exploration, while the Pacific mountains delayed and hindered the exploration of the interior. The Russians were slow to push

Mt. St. Elias. First land seen by Bering.

Cape St. Elias.

their advantage of being the first nation in the field, and their history for the rest of the eighteenth century is chiefly one of exploitation of furs and natives, accompanied by many atrocities. We have to admire the courage and energy of these people, but recall with regret that practically all of their labor was for lust and avarice until after the time of Baranof. They explored some of the coast of Alaska near the present Seward Peninsula in the year 1761 to 1775.

Michael Novidiskoff was probably the first fur trader to follow Bering. He reached Attu, the nearest Aleutian Island to Siberia, in 1745. His success was followed by many others, all like himself merchants and fur traders rather than sailors and none interested in scientific observation. Such traders gradually extended their sway in the face of great danger, as evidenced by the fact that one ship in every three was lost, yet as many as twenty ships a year visited the islands. Their sway was completed by the establishment of a permanent settlement on Kodiak Island in 1783.

After the opening of the nineteenth century, Russian exploration took on new life under the influence of the visionary Czar Alexander the First. Captain Von Krusenstern was sent upon a voyage around the world from 1803 to 1806. While he did not explore Alaska he turned the minds of Russian statesmen to that land once more. Golovnin in 1807, Otto Von Kotzebue in 1815 and Etolin in 1820 all explored the coast of Alaska chiefly in Bering Sea and the Arctic Ocean. Meanwhile the interior was being opened up by Malakoff in 1835 and Zagoskin in 1843, both men confining their operations to the Yukon River which they ascended as far as Nulato where the great river bends east and southward. A few years later the Hudson Bay Company traders descended the Yukon to the mouth of the Tanana River, thus completing the navigation of the Yukon by white men. The only other noteworthy interior exploration of the Russians was that of Lieutenant Nasilef to the Kuskokwim in 1829.

Meanwhile, the other countries were far outstripping the Russians. The chief motive for the early voyages of western Europeans was the perpetual search for the famous Northwest Passage. This search almost rivaled that of the Holy Grail in its perpetual lure and in the number of victims that it claimed. Back in 1576 Sir Martin Frobisher was probably the first noted explorer to seek the Northwest Passage and give it national significance. The English desired such a passage to compete with Spain in the trade of the Indies. This motive was uppermost until the nineteenth century when the passage was sought in the true spirit of exploration so that the white man might know all about the world in which he lived. The search has not been devoid of profit in that it has enabled us to determine the location of the magnetic poles and has answered many of our barometric problems as well as those of interoceanic circulation, tidal action and so forth. Materially, it advanced the whaling era which has alone produced more than $600,000,000 and provided the impetus to Anglo-Russian trade. Frobisher was followed by Davis, Weymouth, Knight, Hall, Hudson, Baffin and Cook, to mention only a few of the intrepid explorers who gave the best years of their lives and even their lives to this search.

Sir John Franklin in 1847 came within 90 miles of completing the Northwest Passage and it has been rightly said that his party forged the last link of the passage with their lives. The search was not to be culminated successfully until 1906 when Roald Amundsen successfully sailed from the Atlantic to the Pacific in his vessel the "Gjoa." The voyage of Captain James Cook, already a world navigator, to the northwest coast in 1778 resulted in the naming of Cape Prince of Wales, Icy Cape and other points. He sailed into the Arctic Ocean until stopped by the ice barrier. His work was so accurately done that it was not altered by many generations of far better equipped navigators. Captain Beechy in 1826 carried on Cook's work and named Point Barrow. Captains Meares, Portlock and Dixon were among the better known English navigators who explored the coast of southeastern and southwestern Alaska in the last decade of the eighteenth century. Their work was consummated by that of George Vancouver, one of Cook's lieutenants. He revisited Alaska in 1791 and explored and accurately charted most of this region. His observations remained the basis of our knowledge of the Pacific Coast regions of Alaska for one hundred years and ranks as one of the outstanding achievements of Alaskan exploration.

Spain was in the most favored position to explore the whole Pacific coast of North America, as she was firmly established in Mexico in the seventeenth century; but whether from inertia or false notions as to the wealth of the northern countries she was singularly backward in pushing her domains beyond California. There are unauthenticated reports of two voyages to the northwest—that of De Fonte from Mexico in 1708, and Juan de Fuca to the straits that now bear his name, in 1592. De Fonte, whose recital is doubted, mentions meeting two traders from Boston in the vicinity of the present coast of British Columbia. In the period between 1774 and 1794 Spain explored extensively in southeastern Alaskan waters. The best known explorer was Bodega Quadra, who sailed to the present site of Sitka in 1775 and explored the coast line. His first voyage was made in the "Sonora," a boat only 36 feet long. He made a second voyage in 1779 and was on intimate terms with Vancouver during his stay in the region.

The English and Spanish navigators clashed at Nootka Sound, a small bay on the western coast of Vancouver Island, in 1789. This had already become a trading center for at least four nations at this time, and the clashes arising from Spain's attempt to control this depot resulted in international complications. Louis XIV of France, in his effort to be the great monarch of the world, sent explorers to all parts. The sole tangible result in Alaska was the voyage of LaPerouse in 1786, covering southeastern Alaska.

The present owners of Alaska were the last to enter the field. It was not until 1798, when Captain Gray discovered the Columbia River, that America really turned attention to Alaska. Previous to this her Yankee traders had probably been frequently seen in the northwest, though we have meager reports of them. The Englishman, James Hanna, in

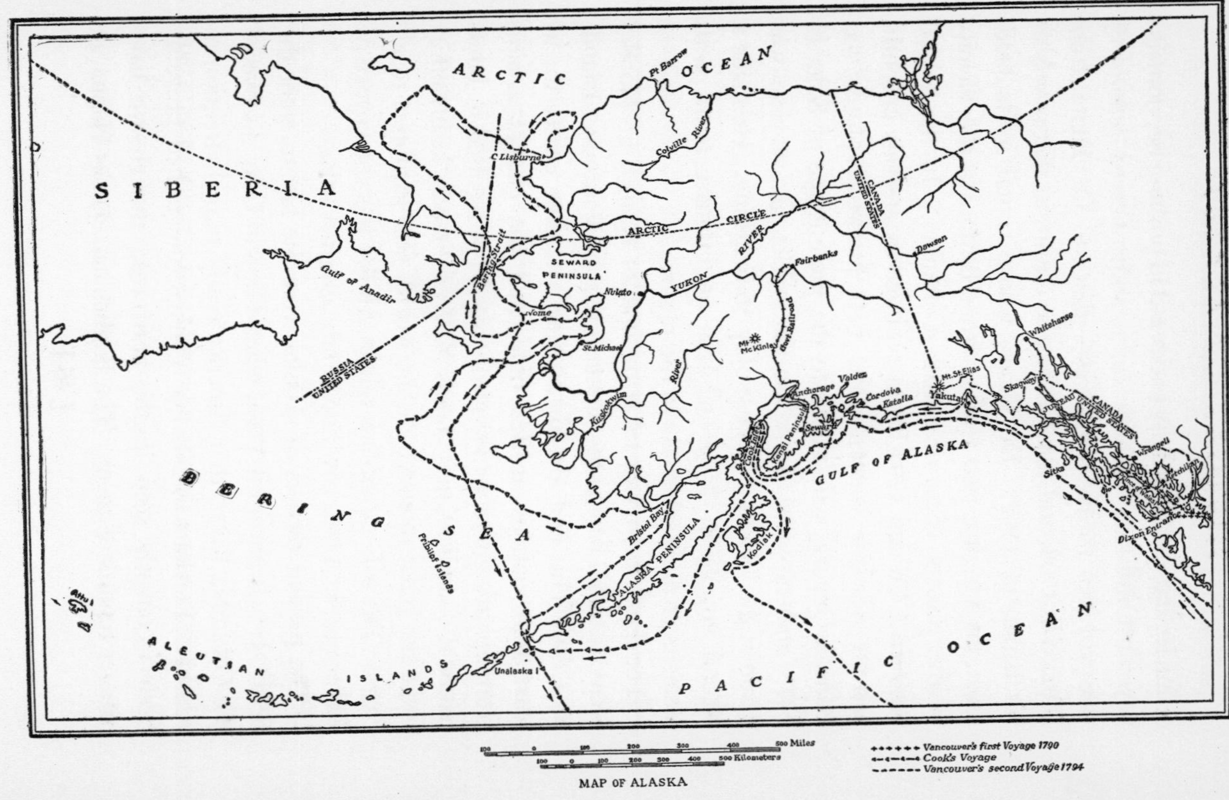

MAP OF ALASKA

1785 had gathered a cargo of sea otter skins near Nootka Sound which he disposed of in China for over $20,000. England and America were both quick to see here the importance of establishing a triangular trade which was to vie in importance with that of the Colonial triangular route from New England to Africa to the West Indies. Here a ship from the home country could stock with civilized materials, deliver them to the northwest Indians for furs, and sell the furs to the Chinese for oriental spices. Unfortunately the original cargo was too often rum and firearms. The journal of one of the Yankee sailors, or "Boston men" as they came to be known in Chinook jargon, reads like a fairy tale. Here in this wild country thousands of miles from civilization he speaks in a matter-of-fact way of meeting numbers of ships and of anchoring in a harbor with five other vessels. The particular ship that he sailed on was sold at Sitka to Baranof for $75,000 and a sloop, on which the intrepid sailors continued on to China while the captain went overland to Russia to return to Boston after several years. These traders and sailors seemed to have sailed around in the wild Pacific in shallops as though it were a lake.

John Jacob Astor had established a company at Astoria in 1811. This became the Northwest Company in 1813 and the Hudson Bay Company in 1821. Astoria, because of this settlement, became an outfitting outpost for the northwest traders.

The exploration of Alaska is far from a closed chapter to-day. Only recently Captain Wilkins flew over 10,000 miles of previously unexplored land in the far north. It has been a country which tried the soul of even the boldest navigator, and its geographical features to-day are a fitting memorial to many of the noble men who have opened the country to civilization. To list such places is to recall pages of history of self-denial and daring. Kennecott Mine, Point Barrow, Cook Inlet, Dixon's Entrance, Quadra Bay, Cape Camaano, Malaspina Glacier, Cleveland Peninsula, Wrangell Island, Kotzebue Sound and such places are a small inkling of this honor roll.

CHAPTER IV

RUSSIAN OCCUPATION

ENOUGH has already been said of the promishleniki and other early Russians in Alaska to show that their rule there was anything but cultured and barely deserved the term civilized. The fact that practically every vessel sent to exploit the Alaskans of their furs was owned by a different individual made cut-throat competition the order of the day, with the Indians and the native Alaskan products the chief sufferers. This was the condition of affairs when Gregor Shelikoff headed a trading voyage of three ships to Kodiak Island in the last decade of the eighteenth century. Observing conditions there he combined his interests with those of another merchant adventurer, Golikoff, and, leaving affairs in the hands of his lieutenants, returned to St. Petersburg. His arrival in the capital was fortunate in that the rulers of Russia had reached the point of such impatience with conditions in Russian America that they were on the point of stopping all trade in Alaska due to these abuses. Shelikoff managed to secure a charter giving his company favorable privileges for their operations in Alaska. His next task was to find a personality strong enough to take over the government of the company in the pioneer lands. His choice fell on Alexander Baranof, a Russian dry-goods salesman, who had just become bankrupt by the failure of a trading operation in Siberia. Shelikoff returned to Russian America and there overcame the last opposition of rival traders as represented by the Lebedoff Company in Cook Inlet. He died in 1795, and should really receive the credit as the founder of the Russian American Company which received exclusive control of Alaska in 1799.

This company was originally capitalized at a half million dollars and later at a million dollars. Its earnings for the first twenty years of its existence were almost six million dollars. The home office of the company was at Irkutsk in Siberia until 1799, when it was transferred to St. Petersburg, and the Emperor, Alexander the First, was made a stockholder. This stretch of thousands of miles between the home office and the field of operations was a tremendous handicap for the company traders, especially when western European nations entered the field in competition with them. Furs had to be shipped to the home office and from there distributed to Europe or China. This disadvantage was further increased by the fact that the Company had to receive all its supplies from Siberia. Other nations could operate on the triangular trade route already described. The company organized Alaska into six districts. Its word was the sole law of the country. The Aleuts were used as slaves and the other natives were practically enslaved or in large part hostile. Company governors filled their reports to the home office with bitter complaints of the unfair tactics of rival nations but the history of their own agents does not bear comparison. It is probable that these handicaps would have seriously hampered the success of the Russian American Company had not Shelikoff hit upon the outstanding personality of the Russian occupation of Alaska as the company governor.

Alexander Andreevitch Baranof came to Alaska with practically every conceivable handicap. He was not of noble birth nor was he connected with the government official family and consequently was despised by the upper castes of Russian society, even after he was ennobled for his work in Alaska. He started with disorganization of the wildest sort. On his way to his post of duty in 1791, he was shipwrecked and forced to recoup enough materials from the wreck to resume his journey. The sea otter was practically exterminated from the Aleutian Islands; the Indians were universally hostile; he had no available money, and was at one time five years without a supply ship. His aides were practically all drunkards and incipient mutiny was a common occurrence. After years of faithful and brilliant duty in Alaska he sickened of his task and resigned but his resignation was at first refused. When finally it was accepted, two of his successors were lost on their way to Sitka. Yet in the face of all these difficulties Baranof showed his company managers a larger profit in the way of dividends than his successors and extended Russian domains to their widest points. He established a factory at Ross in California and seriously considered seizing the Sandwich Islands before he resigned in 1818.

He has been described as a coarse, shrewd, unfeeling despot who ruled his ruffians in Alaska according to his own iron law, working on the motto that "God is in Heaven and St. Petersburg is a long way off." Visitors to his capital at Sitka, however, speak highly of his hospitality and of his enterprising energetic personality. He was probably no worse than those with whom he worked and very possibly somewhat better. He was given to carousals of the wildest sort and was undoubtedly loose in his relations with women. But he was shrewd enough never to allow his excesses to interfere with his business. Baranof did new things in new ways in a pioneer country. He was quick to adapt the wilds to his uses. He thought nothing of securing turpentine from the trees, iron from the hills, and when his pay ship was lost he had the Aleutian women make gay parkas out of bird plumage to pay the hunters. He encouraged the efforts of Russian missionaries and built churches and schools, but his pride and joy were his shipbuilding ways from which he launched fourteen vessels during his residence in Alaska. When he found the hunting grounds of the Aleutian Islands nearly exhausted he was quick to see the advantages of southeastern Alaska and moved his capital from Kodiak to Sitka in 1802. From here his ships and men went to all parts of the Pacific. His traders frequently visited Hawaii, Mexico and Japan. He saw the handicaps under which Russian trade operated as compared with the English and American and did not scruple to encourage any joint trading and hunting enterprises with the foreigners. He frequently bought vessels with their cargoes from these more fortunate traders. In 1812 he entered into a commercial agreement with Astor for their mutual benefit. Finally, in 1818, the Russian Navy succeeded in supplanting Baranof and he returned to Siberia to die at the age of seventy-two on his way to the capital.

Shelikoff as the founder, and Baranof as the guiding genius, were the two factors most influential in the establishment of Russia in North America. Under the Navy, the whole policy of Russia was changed—the foreigner was barred instead of used for the profit of Russia. The ukase of 1821 attempted to close the coast of North America north of 51° to 100 miles off shore. At the same time the company was given a new charter. Such high-handed tactics aroused immediate and bitter opposition from the English and Americans who had already developed a substantial trade in the southeastern islands. England had taken steps to establish a post at Wrangell in 1802, but had been ejected by the Russians in 1811. The English traders, along with those of America, operating out of Nootka Sound were welcome visitors to all of the natives because they brought them better articles of trade and gave them better prices for their furs. Eastern Europe, represented by the Russian American Company, had now expanded to the point where it came into collision with western Europe represented by the Hudson Bay Company. The question of priority either by trade or by exploration did not enter into the clash so much as the strength of the respective home nations. Russia was forced to give way before both countries. In 1824, the United States and Russia entered into an agreement whereby we were given equal trading privileges for ten years, north of 54° 40′, where a boundary line was drawn. A similar treaty was drawn with England in the following year. Thus Russia in America under the Navy lost ground.

Exploration and improved treatment of the natives were, however, encouraged especially under such an able company governor as Baron Wrangell. The establishment of Fort Ross in California in 1812 has already been mentioned. Russia did not recognize Spain's sovereignty north of San Francisco, consequently Baranof felt justified in sending Kuskoff to the northern shores of California with ninety-five Russians and eighty Aleuts. The fort established there was named Ross as a contraction of Russia. The establishment never received permission from Spain or any other country. They were told to leave in 1814, and Spain continually protested their residence there, but kept up a contraband trade, as they felt that the Russians were too strong to oppose by force. The fort grew to a population of about 400, ships were built and food supplies were sent north to Sitka. Baron Wrangell visited Ross in 1833 and then resigned his government of the Russian American Company to negotiate with Mexico for the sale of the land at Ross. The negotiations failed and the company decided to abandon the fort. It was offered for sale to the Hudson Bay Company, but refused, as the English feared the displeasure of California and the United States. Mexico also refused to buy the factory and the Russians finally sold it to John A. Sutter, famous as the owner of the mill near which California gold was discovered in 1849. Sutter bought all of Russia's interests in California for $30,000 and the Russians left in 1842.

Some idea of life in Alaska under the Russians [1] is recorded by a picture of Sitka during these times. When Baranof left in 1818 there were about 400 people in the village, of whom half were Russians and the remainder creoles (part Russian and part Indian), or Aleuts. Just previous to the sale of Alaska in 1867 there were about 1,000 Russians and creoles at Sitka, of whom only 50 were Russian women. A garrison of 200 soldiers were kept in the town with sentries walking their beats night and day. Baranof Castle, the only castle in North America, was built in 1836. A light in the tower was the only aid to navigation on the entire coast of Alaska for more than a century.

The chief industry of the Russians was the fur trade but they felt the need of developing other industries to present a more attractive picture to the home office. There were saw mills, flour mills, tanneries and iron foundries. They manufactured their own bricks and candles, raised potatoes, and entered into a contract with an American concern in 1852 whereby a thousand tons of ice were shipped yearly to California. From 1855 to 1860, 3,000 tons of ice were shipped annually at seven dollars a ton. Mining was started under Peter Doroshin but did not advance to any great extent.

Such a picture would seem very attractive at first glance but aside from fur trading, Russia failed utterly to see the real wealth of Alaska. The treaties of 1824 and 1825 continued in force until 1835 when American traders were forbidden further intercourse with Alaska because of their alleged abuse of the treaty clauses.

[1] C. L. Andrews—Sitka.

The English, through their chief agency, the Hudson Bay Company, foresaw their exclusion from this trade also and determined to forestall it by holding part of the territory by force. They established Fort Simpson just south of the boundary on Dixon's Entrance without opposition. Ogden was sent to the mouth of the Stickine River to establish a fort there in 1802, but the Russians, hearing of their designs, sent a force there to prevent the English from landing, and Zarambo built a fort at Wrangell near the mouth of the river to hold the territory. The English protested against this show of force and the Russian American Company in reparation granted the Hudson Bay Company a ten-year lease to southeastern Alaska south of Cape Spencer. By this lease the Hudson Bay Company was to pay Russia 2,000 land otter skins annually and to supply the Russians with European goods at London prices. This lease was subsequently renewed from time to time until 1867 when it expired on the eve of our purchase.

Meanwhile, the Hudson Bay Company had established Fort Yukon, eighty miles inside Russian territory, in 1847, and were trading on that great river in defiance of Russian authority down to the sale of the territory. Despite their exclusion in 1835, the Americans were frequent visitors to Alaska through the whaling industry. The first whaler to go through Bering Strait was the American ship "Superior" in 1848. In the following year 154 ships went through the Strait, and the whaling fields of the Arctic Ocean attracted annually large numbers of vessels for the next half century.

Alexander the First, the great visionary emperor of the

Russians, had dreamed of world sway emulating his namesake, and had deluded himself to the extent of dividing the world with Napoleon. Napoleon's continental system killed the Russian Navy aborning. The Crimean War and the increasing gravity of internal problems, such as the serfs, made the burial of Russian commerce an assured fact. Alaska as the sole maritime province of Russia now became a burden.

The Russian American Company had failed to renew their charter in 1863 because they regarded the conditions as too harsh and because the government was dissatisfied with their control. From then on the company operated on sufferance and the control of their monopoly was very precarious. Russian expansion, which had started with Peter the Great and Catherine the Great, and had spread until it covered Poland and Scandinavia to the west, the Black Sea and even Persia to the south, all of Siberia and Alaska to the east, had now reached the point where it was about to collapse of its own weight. The problems of solidifying and subjugating these gains proved impossible for the feudal system of government existing at St. Petersburg. Drastic restriction of territory was the obvious immediate remedy necessary. Everything pointed to a complete change in the affairs of Russian America.

Despite the fact that Russian America was on the continent of North America, its history up to this point has little in it that concerned the United States worried with growing pains nearer home. It was clear by 1860, that Russia would be wise to get rid of her far-flung province even

Baranof Castle, Sitka.

at a financial sacrifice. There were individuals in both Canada and the United States interested in securing such a bargain. Diplomacy and politics in Washington, London and St. Petersburg were to drop the plum into the American lap, although the Hudson Bay Company had been first on the scene.

CHAPTER V

PURCHASE OF ALASKA

BOTH the external and internal affairs of Alaska under Russian domination developed in such a way as to make the country less and less attractive to Russia either as an investment or as an extension of her empire. Meanwhile, the march of events in Russia itself was such as to make her more and more anxious to dispose of the territory in any profitable way. The nineteenth century in Russia opened in a blaze of glory with Alexander the First, the young, visionary, more or less radical monarch on the throne. This curious man was so disillusioned by Napoleon that he became insane and made a complete about face in all his ideas and policies by the second decade of the century. He then launched Russia on a career of reaction and bigotry that was to bring her into conflict with the enlightened nations of Western Europe; while the pogroms within Russia itself were all intensified and embittered by the character of his successor, the Emperor Nicholas. This culmination of events served to place Russia, by the middle of the century, in the unenviable position of being without a friend, except the United States, in Christendom.

In Alaskan external affairs we have already seen how the naval governors of the Russian American Company had sought to bolster their interests by securing the ukase of 1821 which closed Alaska to foreign traders. England and the United States were quick to protest against such broad claims. Their protest arose particularly from the fact that both had developed an extensive trade with the northwest coast, but more especially they protested because in so doing they were following out their policy of joint opposition to the high-handed tactics of the Holy Alliance. Russia was the moving spirit in this alliance and the two great English-speaking nations felt that in opposition to her they were laying down a fundamental policy which was later embodied in the Monroe Doctrine. Their protests were heeded for the moment by the treaties of 1824 and 1825. Through these agreements both countries secured trading privileges in Russian America and in turn recognized Russia's claims to the territory north of 54° 40′. After 1834 the United States was excluded from those privileges, whereas England, through the Hudson Bay Company, continued to enjoy them. This was a particularly irritating state of affairs for the United States.

The Nootka Sound controversy of 1789-95 illustrated the keenness of other countries for this northwest trade. Spain and England almost precipitated a world war over the control of this bay which served as a rendezvous for traders on the northwest coast. It was settled in 1795 in favor of England. In 1846 President Polk had been elected on a platform of "national bombast" exemplified in the campaign cry, "fifty-four forty or fight." His attempt to claim Oregon up to the Russian possessions almost led to an Anglo-American war before a settlement was reached on the present boundary at 49°. Both incidents gave Russia warning that other countries were knocking at her doors ready to disturb her peaceful possessions in America.

The whalers had been gradually going farther afield in search of their prey until the first whaler went through Bering Strait in 1849. The phenomenal catches in the Arctic Ocean made that the center of the industry and by 1857 there were 399 ships there in one season. All of these ships touched at both Alaska and Siberia and while waiting for the ice to open traded extensively along the coasts. Their trade was in the nature of contraband, and as such very aggravating to the ruling country, inasmuch as they furnished the natives with firearms and rum and otherwise contaminated them. It is interesting to note that the Civil War had its echo even in these distant regions. The rebel cruiser "Shenandoah" cruised in the Arctic Ocean in June of 1865 and caused about two million dollars damage to Unionist whalers.

The telegraph had so successfully adapted itself to the uses of civilization that within a generation men were planning to cross continents and oceans with it. The most ambitious scheme was planned by Englishmen to lay a cable across the Atlantic Ocean but this attempt, as well as similar attempts across smaller seas, had uniformly failed so that ten million dollars had been lost in submarine cables by 1861. This repeated failure of foreign lines gave patriotic Americans the idea of projecting an overland line from Newfoundland to Ireland touching at all the capitals of the world. Percy McD. Collins of California was the moving spirit in promoting the Pacific end of this proposed line from

Oregon to Siberia. He pointed out that such a line would aid our whalers and would open oriental trade to the United States. As consular agent of this country in Siberia in 1856 he had secured the coöperation of Russia and England.[1]

The Western Union Company adopted his plans in 1864, and Seward memorialized Congress to allow Collins to carry the line across the United States. The company was organized with a capital of $28,000,000 and it was estimated that the line could be completed with five thousand miles of construction at a cost of about $5,000,000. Collins' plan involved penetration into hitherto unexplored country for thousands of miles. Yet it was far from visionary as the total estimate was only half the sum of money which had already been lost in cables. Moreover, there were longer lines already in existence and there were no especially difficult physical features to be overcome along the route. By 1865, 400 miles had been completed, carrying the line as far as New Westminster, British Columbia, on the American side and as far as the Amur River, in Siberia. In addition there were 1,200 miles in process of completion. The plan called for the line to follow the coast to the head waters of the Yukon, thence down that river to the great bend at Nulato, thence across country to Seward Peninsula at Bering Strait. At this point it was planned to lay a submarine cable of sixty miles to Icy Cape, with anchorages midway on the islands. From here it would be comparatively easy to lay the line

[1] It has been hinted that President Pierce and Stoeckl the Russian Ambassador sent Collins to Siberia as part of Russia's bluff to sell Alaska to the United States in the Crimean War. F. Crosno—Univ. of California, Thesis 1926.

across the plains of Siberia to the Amur River. Major Robert Kennecott, who was familiar with Alaska through his explorations as a naturalist with the Hudson Bay Company since 1860, was placed in charge of the work there. After his death in the field in 1866 he was succeeded by William H. Dall, one of Alaska's earliest historians. The successful laying of the Atlantic cable in 1867 made the plan impracticable as the maintenance cost of a line 16,000 miles long compared to one 2,000 would be too great for competition. The surveys of the Western Union line completed the exploration of the Yukon River and revealed to Russia that the Hudson Bay Company had pushed its trading operations down that river in Russian territory as far as the mouth of the Tanana. Along with these English traders Episcopal missionaries had been working in the region as early as 1851. Thus we find Russian America assailed on all sides by the encroachment of other nations.

Internally, Alaska had been developing in such a way that the mother country recognized that it would either have to change its policy materially or surrender its American possessions. Russia had regarded Alaska as an investment rather than a colony and consequently had vested all her interests there in the Russian American Company. This company's chief interest was in the fur trade because of its great profits with a small capital investment. However, they were at a tremendous disadvantage in competing in this trade with other nations inasmuch as they were forced to ship their furs to Siberia for marketing, whereas other nations could seek the easiest and best markets on the coasts of the Pacific.

This enabled foreign traders to pay higher prices and offer more attractive articles for trade and the Indians were becoming more and more unwilling to treat with their Russian masters. The Hudson Bay Company, organized in 1660, had expanded rapidly and had reached contact with Russian territory by 1794. Internal quarrels in the company had stopped their expansion until the union of the Northwest Company and the Hudson Bay in 1821. Then the English were free to protest against Russia's ukase, and by the treaty of 1824 the company had secured free navigation of all streams which rose in Canada and crossed Russian land en route to the sea. However, when they attempted to take advantage of this clause their expedition to the Stikine River in 1833 was stopped by Russian artillery. This violation of the treaty was disavowed by Russia, but the Hudson Bay Company used their grievances to secure an advantageous lease. This opened to their trade the whole of southeastern Alaska from the southern boundary to Mt. St. Elias, for which they paid the Russian American Company 2,000 land otter skins annually and agreed to supply them with provisions. From their headquarters at Wrangell they were making serious inroads into the Russian fur trade.

Other industries were for the most part sporadic and developed by the Russian American Company chiefly to make their rule seem more acceptable to the home government by giving the appearance of general government. Though the waters teemed with fish the Russians neglected this source of income other than to set up a few salteries to supply home consumption only. Lumbering, farming and shipbuilding were carried on to a very limited extent. The Russians discouraged prospecting and even misrepresented important discoveries as they felt that mining would hurt their fur supplies by attracting too many settlers. Gold was first discovered in Alaska probably in 1832 near the Kuskokwim River. Peter Doroshin was the first Russian to do any mining extensively; he prospected in the Alaskan and Kenai Peninsulas and discovered paying quantities of gold, copper and coal. The first coal mine was started at Port Graham in 1855 with capital supplied by San Francisco and Russian interests. The property was developed fairly extensively and convict labor was imported from Siberia, but when the plant was wiped out by fire the Russians did not see fit to start operations again. The offer of $500 reward by the Government of British Columbia for the first gold discovered in southeastern Alaska, then under lease to the Hudson Bay Company, helped to spur on prospectors, and the first strike was made on the Stikine River in 1861 by Choquette. This led to a small rush to that section later known as the Cassiar. At about the same time C. V. Baronovich had made discoveries in the Karta Bay section of southeastern Alaska. But mining under Russian restrictions could not flourish and was not regarded as a source of profit by the home government.

The Russian American Company, although given a monopoly of the territory and hence held responsible by the home government for the well-being of all the inhabitants, regarded their monopoly primarily as a trading privilege to be exploited for profit alone. As late as 1800, there were only a dozen priests in the whole territory and sixteen deacons. There were schools at Kodiak and Sitka but of the poorest type. In general, the company was guilty of such abuses that when they were aired by Kashevaroff the government decided not to renew the charter after 1862, and the company continued to do business merely because no one forbade them to do so.

The Russian American Company by this time was on the verge of bankruptcy and due to their narrow policy showed no signs of relief. Its stock, which had been worth 500 rubles in 1854, had declined to 75 rubles by 1865. Meanwhile, Russia itself was developing to the southward rather than to the east—hence she [1] "wished to strip herself of all outlying possessions as Napoleon had stripped himself of Louisiana in order to gather her strength for her struggle with England for the control of Asia." All of this goes to show that Russia had numerous valid reasons for wishing to get rid of Alaska. On the other hand, nothing in this early history shows why the United States should desire to buy the country; thus proving baseless the oft-repeated rumors that we had sought to buy Alaska in 1846. It is possible that the jingoistic ideas of Polk on the Oregon question led to big talk about the country. For example, R. J. Walker in accepting the office of Secretary of the Treasury from Polk had written "in the event of success in the Oregon question this would leave no European power upon our Pacific Coast

[1] cf. Hon. Charles Sumner's speech on the Cession of Russian America to the U. S., June 5, 1867, U. S. Senate.

except Russia, whose well-known friendship to us would, it is hoped, induce her then to cede to us her North American territory;" but American designs on this country had gone no further than talk.[1]

The first hint of the sale of Alaska to this country in the Russian archives comes in 1854 and 1855 when the Russian American Company, in an effort to protect Alaska from England in the Crimean War, had arranged the fictitious sale of the territory to a San Francisco concern known as the American Russian Company. A contract with the date of sale and purchase price left blank was sent to the Russian Legation in Washington for approval. Baron Edward de Stoeckl asked our Secretary of State whether he should publish it. Our department thought that England would see the sham and discouraged the idea. The newspapers reported that Russia would sell Alaska but Stoeckl denied the reports. The chief promoter of the sale of Alaska was the Grand Duke Constantine, brother of the Czar and bitter opponent of the Russian American Company. He had suggested its sale as early as 1857 but Foreign Minister Gorchakoff had opposed it. At this time Russia was threatened anew by a projected Mormon migration to Alaska which never materialized.

In 1858-9 Stoeckl was in St. Petersburg on a vacation and agreed with the Foreign Minister that if the United States made a move to purchase the territory it should be seriously considered. In this connection Stoeckl had cited many of the arguments previously mentioned for the sale of the

[1] F. A. Golder, *Purchase of Alaska.*

country, and his arguments had been backed by Admiral Popoff, who painted the evils of company rule and the ill will that the company was creating with the United States. It was his opinion that the United States would inevitably expand from Oregon northward to include it. In 1859, Senator Gwin of California offered Stoeckl five million dollars for Alaska. He professed to speak unofficially for President Buchanan, and Appleton, the Assistant Secretary of State, also affirmed that the President favored the purchase. Russia considered this offer and sent a commission to Alaska to report on conditions there. Their report was very unfavorable to the Russian American Company and Russia was ready to sell but by this time the presidential election and the opening of the Civil War stopped all negotiations.

During the war Russia showed her friendship to the United States in many ways. She vetoed Napoleon III's plan of intervention just as we had opposed concerted intervention in Russia when the Polish question had aroused the opposition of all Europe to her. She sent her fleet to this country in 1863 and we considered it a powerful moral demonstration in favor of the North at a critical stage in the war.[1] The fleet was welcomed with great cordiality on all sides, led by Seward, Secretary of State. Oliver Wendell Holmes had written a song to Russia at this time in which he used the phrase, "Who was our friend when the world was

[1] Russia was said to have loaned 500 sailors to the North under Admiral Farragut in his operations around Mobile Bay; and to have held 150,000 more men at Cronstadt to aid the North if England went actively into the war for the Confederacy. *Portland Oregonian,* Jan. 13, 1907.

our foe." Recent research by Professor F. A. Golder has disclosed ulterior motives for this visit of the Russian fleet. At this time Russia was on the verge of war with England. The government was anxious to have the fleets available for action against England in the event of war and thereby avert their total loss as in the World War when Germany kept them bottled in their harbors throughout hostilities. The Russian plan was to send the Atlantic fleet to New York ostensibly on a good-will voyage and to send the Pacific fleet to San Francisco. Then, when war was imminent, both fleets could be notified and put to sea ready to attack British commerce. The threatened war was averted and the Russian government felt that England backed down largely because of this clever move. Thus Russia, acting for her own interest, had unwittingly been of service to the Northern cause, and the United States at the same time had unwittingly been of service to Russia.

The sale of Alaska was agitated almost immediately after the close of the war. In 1866, Constantine had gone over the Foreign Minister's head to the Emperor and secured action; as a result Russia had decided to sell Alaska on December 16, and sent Stoeckl back to Washington to close the deal at not less than five million dollars. Meanwhile, in this country a fur company had been organized in San Francisco by Louis Goldstone to succeed to the privileges of the Hudson Bay Company lease. Goldstone had carefully investigated Alaskan conditions with three vessels which had explored the country and had made complete reports to him so that he would be ready to bid against the Hudson Bay

Company which he knew was not in the good graces of the Russian American Company.[1]

The San Francisco concern was so enthusiastic that they changed from the original idea of succeeding the Hudson Bay Company to a plan to secure a lease direct from Russia to succeed the Russian American Company. The company included in its membership the Collector of the Port in San Francisco and Judge E. Burke, a brother-in-law of Senator Cole of California. They presented their offer to Baron Stoeckl in Washington and to our Minister in Russia, asking for a twenty-five-year charter, for which they would pay five per cent of their gross earnings. In addition, they agreed to help the natives and perform all other necessary acts. Under the conditions existing in Russia this offer was decidedly unfavorable to the government and we have already seen that they had decided to sell the whole country outright in December of 1866. Nevertheless, Stoeckl had gone so far on his return as to give Senator Cole to understand that the lease was practically closed in terms but not in details. Yet two weeks later he closed the sale of the country to our government and then hinted suavely at a bribe to soothe the injured feelings of the San Francisco concern. Stoeckl had probably used the offer of the California company to get Seward to make the first step in proposing the purchase as his government had preferred to have the initiative come from this country. It is interesting to note at this point that the California company was repaid by both countries later

[1] Goldstone later sued the United States Government for his costs in this exploration which he estimated at $183,700, as he claimed that Stoeckl had used his reports to influence Seward to purchase Alaska.

by becoming the nucleus of the Alaska Commercial Company which in 1870 secured a twenty-year monopoly of the Pribilof Islands and also a lease of the Commander Islands from Russia. Goldstone was the only member of the company left out of this later reward. This incident is but another instance of unsavory tactics in the Alaskan purchase.[1]

In 1866, the legislature of the Territory of Washington memorialized Congress to secure fishing rights in Alaska similar to those enjoyed by eastern fishermen on the Banks of Newfoundland. This was later used by Seward as an example of the desire of the Pacific Coast residents to acquire Alaska but recent research shows that this memorial was the work of a crank newspaper reporter, J. L. MacDonald, and was so little known to the Territory of Washington generally that no paper in the territory even published it.

Seward now offered to buy Alaska. His initial offer is reported by his son to have been five million dollars and Russia's reply was ten million dollars. Other authorities say that Russia asked seven million and that Seward finally came to that price with $200,000 additional to clear up all outstanding obligations of the Russian American Company. President Johnson was cool to the idea but Seward secured the approval of the cabinet as he had unusual control over foreign affairs because of Johnson's troubles with reconstruction. Stoeckl came to Seward's house on the night of March 29, 1867, to report that his government was willing to sign the treaty for $7,200,000. Seward would not allow the matter to rest until the next day as he feared that the special

[1] Farrand in the *Washington Historical Quarterly*, Vol. XIII, Number 2.

session might adjourn at any time and he wished to secure ratification at once. The two parties worked all night and the treaty was drawn up and signed at 4:00 A. M., March 30, 1867. The whole negotiations were carried on in an unusually secretive way and very few written documents remain to describe the stages of it. Stoeckl had justly feared the possible failure of ratification, as a later treaty of Seward's for the Danish West Indies failed of ratification. Seward however, secured the coöperation of Senator Sumner, the Chairman of the Committee on Foreign Relations, and the Senate ratified the treaty by a vote of 37 to 2. Various reasons were assigned for this easy ratification compared to the opposition that all executive proposals met with in Congress at the time. The appearance of any administrative act on the eve of the impeachment of President Johnson was usually enough to guarantee a bitter struggle. Senator Sumner's personal influence no doubt had considerable weight. Sumner at this time wrote his friend John Bright, "Abstractly I am against further accessions of territory but this question was so perplexed by considerations of politics and comity and the engagements already entered into by the government, I hesitated to take the responsibility of defeating it." Hence we see that the man most responsible for the ratification was at best an unwilling friend. In addition the treaty had already been agreed to by Russia, and the Senate probably were hesitant to offer insult to Russia by refusing it at this late date. Senator Cole in his memoirs states that ratification was secured by the argument that the payment of so much gold right after the war would be a gesture to other nations that we were in far better financial status than was actually the case.

Alaska was formally turned over to General Lovell H. Rousseau by Captain Pestchouroff at Sitka on October 11, 1867. By this act Russia had fulfilled her part of the treaty, but the United States had not yet paid the sum agreed upon and was not to do so until the following summer, after a bitter fight in the House for the appropriation.

The friends of the Alaskan purchase were indeed wise not to press the appropriation of the necessary money to complete the contract with Russia, because the summer and fall of 1867, during which the treaty had been successively ratified, proclaimed and, as far as Russia was concerned, consummated, were hectic months in Congress. Reconstruction, with all its bitterness, was being fought out in the Senate and House, culminating in the impeachment and trial of President Johnson. Hence, it is logical in a way that no bill for the appropriation of $7,200,000 was reported in the House until May 18, 1868—six months after we had received the territory at Sitka. General N. P. Banks, as Chairman of the House Committee on Foreign Affairs, reported the bill, and after two weeks' discussion, during which the appropriation was attacked bitterly, it was carried by a vote of 113 to 43. The size of this vote can be chiefly attributed to the work of Thaddeus Stevens, leader of the majority in the House.

A singular feature of the appropriation fight in the House is that Banks and Stevens here supported an administration measure though they were the persistent enemies of Andrew

Johnson and his policies in all other matters. It is possible that Stevens may have supported the measure in the belief that it was Seward's own, but it is illogical to believe that so powerful a man as Stevens would not have known that Johnson also favored the measure, and with this knowledge his nature was vindictive enough to have opposed it as part of his policy of embarrassing the President.

It is singular too that the Washington and Philadelphia daily papers owned by Charles P. Forney supported the appropriation although they were notoriously against Johnson. Add to this the undoubted fact that while Congress appropriated $7,200,000, only $7,065,000 ever reached Russia. From the remaining $135,000 Baron Stoeckl admitted that he paid $3,000 to Forney's brother and $1,000 to a California newspaper man for his support of the measure. This combination of singular unaccountable occurrences lends weight to a memorandum of President Johnson's made after a picnic party with Secretary Seward. The memorandum of course is hearsay, but nevertheless it is difficult to disprove. It recites that Stoeckl had told Seward that he had substantially bribed General Banks, "the incorruptible" Thaddeus Stevens, Charles P. Forney, R. J. Walker and Stanton.[1] There were many rumors of bribery at the time of the appropriation fight and these were considered substantial enough to warrant an investigation by the House. The investigation proved nothing but Seward's testimony before the committee was very guarded. He denied em-

[1] Prof. W. A. Dunning, *Political Science Quarterly*, Sept., 1912, Vol. 27, Number 3: $30,000 to Forney of the *Washington Chronicle*, $20,000 to Walker and Stanton, $10,000 to Stevens, and $8,000 to Banks.

phatically giving bribes personally, but, either consciously or not, dodged all references to any bribes that may have been given by Russia. It is certain from the facts that bribery was indulged in, and the whole attitude of Stoeckl throughout the proceedings lends weight to this conclusion. When the Russian Ambassador left this country he expressed himself as sick of the corruption of Congressmen and other public men and hoped that some day they would be more worthy of the country they represented.

The names of Walker, the former Secretary of the Treasury, whose interest in Alaska dates back to 1846, and of Stanton, both prominent Washington attorneys of the day, appear because of their connection with the Perkins claim. A brief survey of this claim which bulks large in the foreign history of the United States of the period will serve to explain the connection. In 1855 Benjamin Perkins had contracted with Stoeckl and a private agent of Russia, Rakielevicz, to deliver powder and ammunition to Russia. Stoeckl later denied the contract and discredited the Russian agent as a former spy. The case was tried in the New York Supreme Court and Perkins lost. He then took $200 to drop his claims. By 1867, Perkins and Rakielevicz had died but the Perkins heirs saw in the Alaska purchase an excellent opportunity of renewing the claim for $800,000. They secured the coöperation of several Congressmen including Butler, and some newspapers. A Senate judiciary committee investigated the case and dropped it. The Perkins heirs then asked for an arbitration. This was refused and they then took the claim to the floor of the House to block the appropriation of the Alaska purchase until settlement should be made with them. Stoeckl asserted that the Congressmen backing the claim were to receive three-fourths of the $800,000 and the heirs one-fourth. Thaddeus Stevens favored the claim at first and then Seward prevailed on him to oppose it. At one time the claimants had almost referred the whole negotiation to a conference committee which Walker, as lobbyist for Stoeckl, planned "to manipulate." They were finally defeated on the floor of the House and the appropriation voted.

Neither the guilt nor the innocence of the parties involved in this whole unsavory negotiation has been proved but the circumstances are sufficient to make this, for the present at least, another black page in our post Civil War history of public men that was later to come to a climax in accusations that touched Blaine and even President Grant.

As we have already seen there were plenty of reasons as to why Russia acted wisely in disposing of Alaska but our survey shows surprisingly few reasons as to why this country should have purchased it. Aside from the comparatively slight commercial intercourse of the United States traders and whalers with Russian America, there was only one point of contact between this country and Alaska. The world telegraph project of Percy McD. Collins in 1856 had as we have seen included a line through interior Alaska to Bering Strait. This enterprising Californian had lectured throughout the United States on the practical side of his plan and described its route. He had secured congressional attention by a bill in the House in 1861 providing $50,000 for a survey in Russian America. Though the measure failed it brought the country out of obscurity. President Lincoln mentioned the plan in his message of 1864; Seward was a wholehearted supporter of the idea and familiarized himself with Alaskan topography along the route as early as May, 1864. Moreover, every stockholder in the line, after the Western Union took over the rights of Collins, was a student of the route. Finally, this project had accustomed Russia and the United States to official coöperation in Bering Sea as both lent ships and protection to the enterprise. The telegraph for all of these reasons was an agent in acquainting the United States with Russian America but its failure left no tangible reason for purchase of that portion of the route.

There is, furthermore, the obvious reason of the jingos who wished to secure all of North America for the United States. Seward himself was a leader of this group. As a senator he had said that, "the Russian outposts in North America will yet become the outposts of my own country." In 1852 he had spoken for aid to the whalers in the Arctic Ocean and had taken the occasion to say that the Pacific would be the theater of the world's politics in the future, and that the United States should be dominant there. Finally, we have seen his interest in the telegraph line there. The jingoists had even urged that we buy British Columbia and it is said that their pretensions had been stopped only by the Canadian Federation whereby British Columbia was drawn closer to eastern Canada. One curious reason was advanced by "Petroleum v. Naseby" who had said that we should buy Alaska to get rid of the Blairs and other office-seekers by putting them as far away as possible. The reasons listed by Senator Sumner for the purchase were as follows:

1. The desire of the Pacific Coast for fisheries and other privileges.

   We have already seen that the Washington memorial for fishery privileges was the work of an isolated crank and that the fur privileges were the work of a company of exploiters.
2. The refusal of Russia to renew the charter of the Russian American Company.

   This reason, however, does not affect the United States.
3. The friendship of Russia and the United States.

   We have seen that this friendship has been over-emphasized and Professor Golder says there is nothing in Russian archives to show that this affected either state department in the negotiation.
4. The necessity of preventing England from getting it.

   England at this time was afraid to offend the United States as shown by the way in which she accepted the affronts of our Senate in regard to the "Alabama" claims. At that time there was an armed truce in Europe brought about by Bismarck's high-handed tactics and England knew that her attitude in the Civil War had dangerously antagonized this country when she could not afford to risk a war with us.
5. The creation of new industrial interests on the Pacific necessary to the supremacy of our empire on sea and land.
6. To visit and secure unlimited commerce with Japan and China.

The last two reasons as part of our big talk on Manifest Destiny or its equivalent may possibly have weight. They lead us to the inevitable conclusion that the chief reason for the United States buying Alaska was William H. Seward. Whether he was actuated by his desire to aggrandize America and make it all supreme on this continent, as shown by his later efforts toward securing Hawaii, Cuba, Hayti, San Domingo and the Danish West Indies; or whether he wished to sustain our interests in the Pacific by a good base in the Aleutian Islands; or finally whether, as Stoeckl has claimed, he simply wished to curry popularity in his party, will never be definitely determined.

This was a new step in American policy. Hitherto all territory acquired had been contiguous, with the expectation that one day it would form a part of the Union. Alaska was bought with no such idea. Some will say that Stoeckl's open purse was the dominating motive, others will say that it was self-interest. It is certain that it was not done in any spirit of far-sighted policy by the American government, yet by almost stumbling into a treaty, we have wrought far greater than even Seward, its most enthusiastic supporter, ever dreamed.

CHAPTER VI

NEGLECT

THE subsequent history of Alaska for two decades does not raise the prestige of our national government from the veiled blow suffered in the appropriation fight. From 1867 until 1884, if not later, the history of our government, or rather the lack of government in Alaska, is a blot upon our pretensions toward enlightened democracy. The only excuse for the reign of lawlessness and corruption that we encouraged in the country is that Alaska was our maiden experiment in the control of a colony separate from the United States, and possibly that the settlers, released from the old patriarchal rule of the Russian American Company, misused their freedom under the new masters. It is this period of Alaskan history that Kipling refers to when he says: "And there's never law of God nor man runs north of 53."

We have already noted the condition of Sitka at the close of Russian occupation. The picture that we have seen differs greatly from that which existed in the popular fancy when the purchase of Alaska was announced. Newspapers, public speakers, public opinion in general attacked the treaty as the height of folly. It was variously described as: "Seward's Ice-box," "Walrussia," "The playground of the polar bear," etc. Seward's only reply to this flood of sarcasm was to collect some of the things that were said about Louisiana after Jefferson's purchase of that great territory. His point was well taken that the jibes of his own day were as far from the mark as those of 1803. As a matter of fact, Alaska, as we have seen, was an empire in extent with an equable climate for the geographical location of the country. The settlements of which Sitka was the largest resembled that town in general. Kodiak, on the island of that name near the Aleutian Peninsula, was the oldest town though still of only a few hundred population. It was a fur center and also had an ice company which supplied merchants in San Francisco. Unalaska was a coaling station for all ships going from the Pacific into Bering Sea. Wrangell, at the mouth of the Stickine River, was the largest trading village in southeastern Alaska. In addition there were several Indian villages of which the better known to the whites were those in southeastern Alaska such as Yakutat, Kake, Klawack, Kasaan and Port Tongass. The chief industry of the country was furs as it had been under the Russians, and the most prized fur was that of the seal taken on the Pribilof Islands. America knew the value of these islands well, even before the purchase, as shown by the fact that there were at least four companies hunting on the two islands in 1868.

The population in 1867 cannot be ascertained exactly because of the primitive nature of the country. However, estimates place it at about 483 whites, of whom 150 were Americans, 1,500 creoles or half breeds and the rest, about 26,000, Indians. Of this total population about 1,300 were estimated as the total civilized population; the majority of these were far from cultured. They were the rough, hardy,

Sitka in the early days of American occupation.

pioneer element who were, in their own words, "not in Alaska for their health." They visited the country during the best seasons of the year to exploit it in every way possible. They were the roughest side of our countrymen and taught the Indians to despise America early in Alaskan history. The Indian population was made up of a small nucleus of Aleuts, who were now practically all in a state of serfdom; the Esquimaux, fast becoming an easy prey to the contamination of traders; and the Koloshians, a sturdy, peaceable type in southeastern Alaska. All these groups loved whiskey or more properly "hooch," a concoction of molasses, beans, rice, flour or any other commodity that might be at hand which mixed together and fermented would make a sane man crazy with two drinks. These southern natives were not so easily overcome by the whites as the more northern tribes because they were brought up in a warlike atmosphere and were never subjected by the Russians. The Thlingits and Haidas kept the interior natives under their sway and acted as middlemen between them and the whites. When the Hudson Bay Company established posts in the interior, this middle trade was spoiled and the natives burned Fort Selkirk on the upper Yukon in 1852 in retaliation. The Chilkats kept the famous Chilkoot Pass to the interior a secret in the tribe until 1880. This pass route to the Yukon was discovered at that time by Edmund Bean, who led sixteen miners through the pass into the interior.

This was the type of country that had passed from the hands of a declining government, whose colonial policy reflected its internal decline, to a young growing government. But the growth of the United States was so great in its immediate territory that it failed to take note of its only outlying territory and remained an amateur in colonial affairs. Indeed it may still be regarded as an amateur at this time. Alaska's growth will be healthy and strong only when the United States learns the lesson that England learned in the 1840's—that is, she must forget mercantilism completely and adopt a policy of colonial self-determination. Various ideas were advanced as to the means of making the purchase of Alaska useful to our government. It was suggested as a good place for office seekers as it was considered cold enough to dispose of such vermin permanently. It was also seriously proposed as a penal colony. Exile in Alaska, it was pointed out, would be a cheap way of disposing of misfits and at the same time would give the unfortunates an opportunity to regain their lost manhood. It was also proposed that we transport the population of Iceland to Alaska. None of these suggestions, however, were very helpful in solving this new problem presented to our government.

Alaska could not properly be called a colony as that term was avoided by the United States after the Revolution. The term "territory" had become fashionable with the Ordinance of 1787. This, however, had by 1867 come to mean that the country so designated would one day be a state. It was felt that this would not be true of Alaska. From the formation of the Union until 1898, thirty-one states had been admitted to the Union after having been called territories. Alaska was the sole exception to this routine development of new lands. Not knowing just what to do about fixing the status of this unique acquisition, Congress as usual did nothing. The country was variously referred to as district or territory down to this century.[1] It is difficult to draw a clear distinction between these two terms and the distinction, in so far as it relates to Alaska, seems useless. It would be more useful to distinguish between "incorporated and unincorporated" territory or between "organized and unorganized" territory.[2]

Regardless of the term that we use for the status of Alaska there is no doubt that the President and Congress have had practically absolute jurisdiction over the country from the time of the purchase and are bound only by the limitations in the Constitution. Judicial decisions have held that Alaska was an incorporated territory practically from the time of the purchase.[3]

By the purchase treaty Russia had conveyed to the United States all that she had to convey free of all encumbrances. Under Article Three of this treaty all the inhabitants of Alaska, except uncivilized native tribes and those Russians who should return to Russia within three years were "admitted to the enjoyment of the rights, advantages and immunities of citizens of the United States" and were to "be maintained and protected in the full enjoyment of their liberty, property and religion." The uncivilized tribes were to be "subject to such laws and regulations as the United States may adopt." Legally, several questions were raised

[1] Max Farrand, "Territory and District," *American Historical Review*, Volume V, pages 676-681.

[2] G. W. Spicer, *The Constitutional Status and Government of Alaska.*

[3] Rasmussen vs. U. S. 197 U. S. 516.

by this treaty—for example, where to draw the line between civilized and uncivilized, and what government to give the uncivilized. Practically, the only question in the minds of Alaskans was when were they to be maintained and protected in liberty, property and religion. They received no answer to this question for seventeen years and a doubtful answer at best for forty years. The civilized peoples were finally held to be the Russians and Americans and creoles living in Alaska at the time of the purchase, and in addition any natives living apart from their tribes who had adopted the habits of civilized life. The uncivilized were not given any status at all until 1915. Meanwhile, they were not regarded as dwellers in an Indian country and consequently eligible for protection under the reservation system, nor was any way shown whereby they could become citizens. They were loosely held to be "dependent wards." All this held back the development of the territory as the natives were unable to hold land, own mines, or operate ships; though many of them were ready for these things before the end of the nineteenth century.

Civil government was felt to be impossible in Alaska in 1867, as the area was too great and the population too sparse. Furthermore, most of the civilized people were held there by commercial rather than civil ties and the rest were unable to govern themselves. For lack of a better solution our government decided to turn the country over to the Army. For this purpose six posts were established—at Kodiak, Kenai, Sitka, Koutznoo, Wrangell and Tongass. No attempt was made to control the interior or the Bering Sea area. General

Davis in his report of 1868 recommended the Army as the fitting body to precede settlers to Alaska as it would conciliate the Indians and manage them properly. History has shown that Army rule was the absolute antithesis of this promise. The General discouraged the idea of civil government and also the sending of Indian agents to the country as he feared that either step would precipitate a long war. He showed by this report his ignorance of the true character of the Alaskan natives. From 1869 down to 1877, when the Army was supplanted, the annual reports urge again and again that Congress send a steamer to that country for patrol duty and the recommendations were uniformly ignored. The government reports referred to the corruption of revenue officers who exploited the natives and the resources for the benefit of the large trading companies. They also decried the prohibition of liquor. The reports for the most part were very meager. In 1873-74, there were practically no official reports at all, although testimony from other sources shows that these were years of suffering on the part of Alaskans at the hands of the Army.

By 1875, the commanding officers had reached the conclusion that civil government would be a good solution. General Howard was especially bold in this respect and urged at least judges and marshals for the country. He pointed out that the Army was held responsible for the preservation of law and order and yet was denied the legal jurisdiction of an ordinary police force. It was during this period that the so-called bombardment of Wrangell took place on Christmas night of 1869. This consisted merely of the shelling of the Indian portion of the village for two days in order to secure the delivery of an Indian who had murdered one of the white residents. The official reports place the Indians practically entirely in the wrong, whereas, non-partisan stories of the affair show that the Army officers provoked the whole incident by debauching the native women. This incident is mentioned as more or less typical of conditions in Alaska under the Army. Reports on this affair show that all officers agreed that soldiers were useless in Alaska, that Indians and soldiers demoralized and debauched one another. Responsible Americans in various parts of the territory testified to the excesses of the soldiers and their bad influence on the natives.

In response to a Senate resolution of 1876 asking for the report on military arrests in Alaska, the first report listed seventy-five arrests at the two posts of Wrangell and Sitka in three years. This is corrected later to a total of 220 arrests in three years of which at least 200 occurred in Sitka alone. The great proportion of these arrests were for liquor violations. It is significant that "Drunken Lizzie" figures in the list thirteen times. Army rule was foredoomed to failure at the outset. After a year or two five posts were abandoned, leaving Sitka alone, and later Wrangell was added once more, but any attempt to exert control outside of these posts was foolish as the chief mode of transportation in the area was by water. Commanding officers themselves reported that one vessel would have been far better than 500 soldiers. If this were the only charge against the Army we might well forget them but the weight of testimony shows that the Army posts themselves were perhaps more grossly misgoverned than the more remote parts of the territory. The figures above show that the natives would have been better off and many lives would have been saved if the Army had never been there. The officers and men were among the chief offenders in continual drinking and other excesses so that there were probably more troubles in the ten years of Army rule than in any decade of Russian occupancy. The great size of Alaska, the weakness of the Indians and the fact that the soldiers sent there had but recently been released from Civil War discipline, all combined to make this record a sorry one.

The later history of Army rule in Alaska is a more pleasant story. It provided valuable protection to the gold stampeders in '98 and performed great feats of exploration. Lieutenant Schwatka in 1883 was one of the earliest explorers to traverse most of the Yukon River and its tributaries. He was followed by the explorations of Allen in the middle regions of the Yukon and those of Stoney in Kotzebue Sound. All of these records go to show that the Army in attempting to rule Alaska was outside the scope of its proper work. In 1868, Congress had extended the customs laws of the United States to the territory and had also given the district courts of Washington, Oregon and California jurisdiction over offenses committed in Alaska. This latter extension was practically useless as no provision was made for arresting the culprits or for transporting them to the States. These were the only laws passed by Congress for Alaska from 1868 to 1884, and it will be recalled that under our Constitution,

Congress was the only body empowered to care for the needs of the territory.

When the Army left in 1877 the customs collector at Sitka was the sole authority remaining to govern 40,000 people in an area equivalent to the United States east of the Mississippi. The collector had no law to enforce except customs regulations and even these were ham-strung by a conflict of authority in the treasury department so that the customs officers were ordered to stop all liquor importations and the revenue officers were ordered to issue licenses to sell liquor in Alaska. The white residents of Sitka, vastly outnumbered by the Indians, were so terrorized in 1879 by the fear of an Indian uprising that they petitioned Washington for relief. Their calls, however, as usual were unheeded. In desperation they sought aid from the English at Victoria. The British sloop of war "Osprey" was sent to Sitka under Captain A'Court and remained there to keep order until relieved by the steamship "Alaska." The Navy then took control until 1884, ruling most of the time by the ship "Jamestown" stationed at Sitka. Although this was a sailing vessel and hence useless for navigation in the inland waterways, the Navy rule was far better than the Army. Captain L. A. Beardslee organized a provisional government of Sitka which failed because of disagreement among the whites. His second step of engaging prominent natives as provisional police for the Indians proved more successful and by 1884 the control of southeastern Alaska was fairly stable. Serious outbreaks were practically eliminated but anything like the conditions under which we live was not approached. There

U. S. S. "Jamestown," warship which governed Alaska 1879-84.

was no legal title to land, murderers and robbers might go unpunished, children could not inherit estates, and any order that might be enforced was accomplished by usurpation of authority.

If any mistake worse than the others could be picked out of this period it would be the absurd attempt to enforce prohibition. The importation of good liquor was forbidden and consequently whites and natives alike turned to distillation of "hooch" or equally bad rum. The population of 1,700 whites and Indians in Sitka alone used over a hundred barrels of molasses a month. One customs collector estimates that there were about a dozen sober people in the town. The Indians were peaceable and tractable so long as they were sober, but under the influence of hooch they became so many maniacs. Ex-soldiers were prosperous saloon-keepers, a commentary on the type of rule Alaska had in its first decade under the United States. Even missionaries and government officials were engaged in the traffic. Smuggling from British Columbia was rampant as the light draught vessels could easily escape the clumsy government patrol boats. As much as 60,000 gallons of liquor were said to have been smuggled from Canada in the year 1898 alone. As we have seen, the customs department was seeking to enforce prohibition while the revenue officers taxed 112 dealers in 1896, 147 in 1897 and 373 in 1898. Juneau had forty saloons and Skagway one hundred and four. Yet in the four years from 1895 to 1898 close to $150,000 was spent in enforcing prohibition.

Although our government was slow to recognize that we

had acquired a northern territory of such proportions as to constitute almost an empire, our private citizens were quick to realize the value of the territory. Hutchinson, Kohl & Co. of San Francisco had accompanied our officials to Sitka in 1867 and had purchased the commercial holdings of the Russian American Company at the time when the Army was taking over the government property. The assets of these merchants were later secured by the Alaska Commercial Company which obtained a twenty-year lease to the Pribilof Islands in 1870. Although the lease of this company referred to two small islands, the control of the company was practically a monopoly over Alaskan trade through the connivance of revenue officers in discouraging other traders. Bitter tirades were launched against the corruption of this monopoly. While these attacks were probably far from the truth it is noteworthy that several of the early government agents in Alaska were later officers of the Alaska Commercial Company and the Collector of the Port in San Francisco was a prime mover in its affairs. The company had powerful friends, even in Congress—Senator Cole of California, for example, was related to large shareholders and was especially active in securing favors for these merchants. The means whereby they secured their lease were themselves rather dark. It was brought out later that the company's bid for the lease was favored over higher offers and in the face of legal decisions against them. It was even charged that a brother-in-law of President Grant was made a member of the company to secure additional favor. Their dividends ran into millions of dollars and charges were rife that they discouraged settlement of the territory to protect their fur interests and also routed all intercourse with the territory through San Francisco to protect their trade monopoly. It was rumored that in the twenty years that the company controlled the Pribilof Islands they sold three million skins although by the terms of the lease they were to kill a hundred thousand seals a year.

The whaling industry continued to grow despite the severe disasters of 1871 and 1876, which destroyed as many as forty ships in one storm. But by 1880 the industry began to decline due both to the growing scarcity of whales and to competition in the Arctic Ocean. Salmon fishing, which had been merely a means of providing fish for the local residents under Russian rule, soon broadened into an exporting business. The first American saltery was set up in 1868, and the first cannery began operations at Klawack on Prince of Wales Island in 1878. By 1898, there were fifty-five canneries operating in Alaska, and most of the great corporations which now control the industry—such as the Alaska Packers' Association, the Northwestern Fisheries, Libby, McNeil and Libby and the Booth Fisheries—were in the field.

The Stickine gold excitement of 1861 led to several other strikes in the vicinity of Wrangell and the Cassiar, and these in turn to the discovery of the Juneau Mines, notably that of Treadwell in 1893. This mine, for many years one of the greatest gold mines in the world, continued operations down to 1917. The stories of mining in this section are many and varied. A bitter fight arose between Dick Harris and Joe Juneau, the joint discoverers, over the naming of the new region. It was finally compromised by naming the town Juneau, and the mining district Harrisburg. In 1886, the miners of Juneau and Treadwell, exasperated by the importations of oriental labor, packed all the Chinese of the district, except a favorite pioneer, China Joe, into two small boats and shipped them to Wrangell. Governor Swineford tried vainly to get them back but desisted when the miners threatened to line the beach with shot guns to receive them. The mineral production of this period centered in southeastern Alaska but the rest of the territory was being opened slowly. Gold was first discovered on the Tanana River in 1878 and by 1883 there were several hundred prospectors in the Yukon. Coal had been discovered at Cape Lisburne in 1881, and at Kachemak Bay in 1888.

Thus economically Alaska was forging ahead under American initiative, but governmentally she remained essentially a neglected country. This neglect must be attributed chiefly to Congress but Alaskans themselves were certainly somewhat at fault through their lack of unified demands. The divergent interests and the wide separation of centers of white population made a concerted campaign for reform almost impossible. The only newspapers expressing the ideas of the territory were published in San Francisco. The chief sources of information at Washington were either agents of the Alaska Commercial Company or professional lobbyists or government officers who professed themselves to be experts on Alaskan affairs after visits there of a few months. The other means of making known their needs was typically Anglo-Saxon, through conventions held for the

Treadwell Mine in early days.

most part in southeastern Alaska. As early as 1880, Colonel M. D. Ball, Collector of Customs at Sitka, and head of the abortive provisional government that had been set up there, was sent as a delegate to Washington but he received little or no attention there. Approximately twenty-five bills were presented to Congress in the years 1869-1880, with a view to providing some sort of government for the territory. They were all shelved or lost in futile debate as to what kind of government should be given Alaska, the legislators failing to note that meanwhile they were giving no government at all. Objections were raised that Alaskan government should not combine executive and judicial duties in one person as such practice was not considered good form in the United States. Railroads were proposed from the interior of Alaska down through the islands and were defeated not so much on the reasonable objection that such a plan would be too expensive but on the ignorant objection that a railroad would not be able to operate more than six months in the year.

The first legislation looking toward establishing government in Alaska was the Organic Act of 1884. This act referred solely to the administration of justice. There was no legislative power granted to Alaska for forty-five years and for thirty-nine years the territory was without an official agent at Washington to make known its needs. The Act of 1884 provided for one district court such as those of the United States, with a judge appointed by the President to hold at least two terms of the court in each year—one at Sitka and another at Wrangell—and such special sessions as were necessary. In addition the President appointed a district attorney, a marshal and four commissioners. The marshal was the executive officer of the court and was directed to provide four deputies to reside at Sitka, Wrangell, Unalaska and Juneau, along with the commissioners. The act also extended the general laws of the State of Oregon to Alaska "as far as they were applicable and not in conflict with the laws of the United States."

This act was a great step forward but the eleven officials set up under it were faced with the practically impossible task of carrying out the powers conferred upon them. The chief hindrances facing them were:[1] the inadequate number of officials, the lack of mail and transportation facilities, the difficulty of securing competent juries, adverse public sentiment toward prohibition, the uncertainty of the applicability of the laws of Oregon, and the fee system of compensating officials. In 1890, there were about 300 villages and towns in the territory, some of which were at least 3,000 miles from the nearest commissioner. During all the latter part of the last century there was no mail communication except with a few towns in southeastern Alaska and even here monthly mail was the best service. One example will serve to show some of the difficulty attending the administration of justice. If a crime were committed in Unalaska the appeal of the litigant must be heard in Sitka, 1,200 miles away, and the only way to reach this town was by way of San Francisco, a distance of nearly 4,000 miles each way.

Some of the handicaps under which the officials labored may be gleaned from the requests of the United States

[1] Spicer, *Status and Government of Alaska,* page 50.

Marshal for Alaska who asks: for appropriations for court houses and jails, for the opportunity to execute his bond, and even for traveling expenses. Because of the unpopularity of prohibition it was practically impossible to get a grand jury to indict or a petit jury to convict persons charged with its violation. The people of Alaska took the position that Congress passed the prohibition law for the Indians and not for the whites and consequently felt justified in opposing it. This act of 1884 remained practically the sum total of Congressional legislation for Alaska until the gold rush of 1898 brought the country before the attention of the world. The bulk of the territory got along as best it might. Most of the inhabitants were fortunately law-abiding; and for those who were not, the "Miner's law" of death or banishment provided quick and sure punishment either by humans or by the animals and mosquitoes. Alaska in spite of the restrictions of poor government or no government at all and monopolistic control of industry was developing as well as any pioneer territory could but the next few years were to bring tremendous changes. The Klondike discovery reawakened adventure, and the desire for quick wealth in all parts of the world brought its seekers in hordes to Alaska.

CHAPTER VII

THE "RUSH" ERA

THE nineteenth century history of North America has been powerfully affected by a geologic strata that runs along the Pacific Coast of the Rocky Mountains from the Gulf of California to Bering Sea. This strip has been the scene of successive rich gold discoveries, each of which led to stampedes, and affected the history of each country in which they were located, and also served as a magnet to draw adventurous spirits from the more settled portions of the continent. Such rushes have occurred in New Mexico, in California in '49, in Colorado near Denver, in the Coeur d'Alene Idaho region, in British Columbia along the Fraser and Cassiar Rivers, in the Yukon territory at Atlin and the Klondike, and finally in Alaska from Forty Mile Creek down the Yukon and its tributaries, culminating at Nome on the shores of Bering Sea in 1900.

The more important of these stampedes were so closely grouped chronologically that many pioneers figured in most of them. The life of Alexander "Buck" Choquette is typical. Born in eastern Canada he rushed across the plains to California in '49 as a boy in his teens. From there he went north to Victoria, B. C., where he took part in the Fraser River excitement of '59. He left that to go still farther north to the Stickine River, or Cassiar, where he discovered the first gold in '61 and took a leading part in the '74 rush there. Some of his fellow miners from the Cassiar went on to Juneau to make their strike in '81 that led to the Treadwell Mine. As an old man, Buck Choquette rushed to the Klondike in '98 and succumbed to the hardships of that stampede. His sons went on down the river to take part in the Nome rush of 1900.

The first gold excitement entirely confined to Alaska was that of 1881 in Juneau and Douglas. Joe Juneau and Dick Harris discovered gold on both sides of Gastineau Channel and sold their interests on Douglas Island to John Treadwell of San Francisco, who combined the deposits of four mines into the great Treadwell group which from 1885 to 1915 ranked as one of the world's largest gold mines. For a generation two hundred and forty stamps at this mine kept at their task of grinding ore day and night throughout the year. The owners were wise enough to see the opportunities for big profits in a very low grade ore by combining low transportation and low mining costs with mass production. They mined over 250,000 tons of ore a year and in their generation of activity turned over a profit of close to $20,000,000 to their owners. These profits did not affect Alaskan history so much as the fact that Treadwell employed between two and three hundred men throughout this early period at an average wage of $2.00 to $2.50 per day and board. By doing this the mine takes rank in Alaskan history as the greatest "grub staker" of them all, and may be justly considered a great force in the opening up of Alaska's mineral wealth. Newcomers, or "cheechackos," were introduced here to Alaskan life and inoculated with the gold fever. Old timers, or "sourdoughs," drifted back to this mine to recoup their finances for another try.

The earliest real prospecting in interior Alaska was that of George Holt on the Yukon in the '70's. His work, however, was very much of a lone effort because of the difficulties of reaching the interior from tide water. The best passes to the Yukon were at the head of Lynn Canal and were all controlled by the warlike Chilkat Indians who jealously guarded their monopoly of trade with the interior Stick Indians. They not only repelled all attempts to go through their passes but even kept the routes of Chilkoot and White Pass secret. Captain Beardslee, the first naval officer in command in Alaska, managed to secure coöperation from the Chilkats so that Edmund Bean and his party went over the Chilkoot Pass in 1880. The work of Col. Sol Ripinsky at Haines was a great factor in keeping the Chilkats law abiding in later years. By 1883, the Cassiar rush on the Stickine had produced about $5,000,000 and two thousand or more prospectors there were looking for less exhausted fields. The first comers to the Yukon prospected on the Lewes and Stewart Rivers. Forty Mile Creek was discovered by Franklin in 1886—the first rich strike. By '93 two hundred miners in the Yukon had taken out an average of $1,000 each from their placer workings. By '96 there were 1,760 miners in that region and the total production was about one million dollars.

One of these early prospectors was George Carmack, born in California in 1860 and attracted to Alaska by the Juneau discoveries of '81. From there he started on his prospecting in the Yukon which for eleven years did not return as much profit as his fur trading and fishing. In this period, like many of his fellows, he became a squaw man. He was a sober, level-headed, typically sourdough type; and was probably more of a hunter than a miner. In the summer of 1896, in company with Skookum Jim and Tagish Charlie, his Indian intimates,[1] he was prospecting and fishing on the upper Yukon in Canada, in the vicinity of the Klondike River. Robert Henderson, a Scotsman, had been prospecting on the upper parts of the same river and had made a fair strike which he hastened down river to record, telling Carmack, among others, about it on the way down. Carmack then went up to Bonanza Creek where he made his great strike on July 26, 1896, and the three prospectors using two fry pans panned out $700,000 in gold from the claim. Carmack failed to tell Henderson of his great luck, and the latter bucked misfortune for several years by working on the wrong claims. He finally left the scene of one of the world's greatest gold strikes in which he was if not the first, certainly one of the most deserving discoverers, a penniless man. The scene of these great discoveries is an area of about 800 square miles comprising the Klondike River and the numerous deep cut streams leading into it. The whole area is dominated by the "great Dome" rising about 3,000 feet above the surrounding country. From this eminence creeks flow out on all sides, like a hub and the spokes of a wheel, all leading down to the Yukon River at the present

[1] Valdez' Number "Pathfinder."

site of Dawson. It is a rectangular strip, about 30 x 40 miles running east and west, rather than circular and lies entirely within the Yukon territory in Canada, being about fifty miles east of the Alaskan boundary.

While Carmack was not the first to discover gold in the Klondike, to him must go the honor of discovery as his strike was the dramatic incident that started the great stampede of 1898 and affected all portions of the world. The first result was a quiet rush to the vicinity by prospectors along the upper Yukon in '97. Most of these struck it rich and a few made fortunes. It was over a year before the outside world awakened to the report of a new El Dorado and the bulk of the outsiders failed to get any more for their trouble than experience. The days of '49 were lived over again but the conditions of '49 were far different—sadly so for the majority of green stampeders. The steamship "Excelsior" tied up at San Francisco on June 16, 1897, and the local papers carried the story of a handful of prospectors who carried down the gangplank three-quarters of a million dollars in gold dust. This story, however, did not catch the imagination of the world so much as the clever phrase of a Seattle reporter who described the arrival of the steamship "Portland" on the 17th, with $800,000 in dust as a ship bringing "a ton of gold." Almost at once all available vessels were overwhelmed with applications for passage. Both new and old boats were requisitioned by transportation companies eager to reap the easy money of gold-mad people. Inter-city rivalry combined with the flood of transportation company advertising to make the Klondike a household word

S. S. "*Portland*" *arriving in Seattle, Washington, with "ton of gold,"* June 17, 1897.

throughout this continent. San Francisco, Portland and Seattle in the United States vied with one another and with Vancouver and Victoria in Canada. Every town within two thousand miles of the Klondike advertised itself as a take-off point for Yukon gold and attacked the claims of its rivals.

At least six routes were prominently mentioned—Canadian Overland, the Stickine, Taku, Dalton Trail, White Pass, Chilkoot Pass and the Yukon via St. Michael's. All but the last three of these were well nigh impossible considering the type of stampeder that was to tackle them, but this did not deter the cupidity of transporation agencies. Some idea of the advertising campaign may be gained from that carried on by Seattle. The Chamber of Commerce of that city used millions of newspapers for their advertising as well as a broadcast of circulars and canvassing. The rush would have been the greatest in history had not the Spanish War broken out in 1898 to deter many of those wavering at that late date. It has been estimated that between 200,000 and 300,000 people started for the Klondike and that close to 50,000 actually reached the interior of Alaska and Canada. The cost of reaching the Klondike, depending on the type of outfit carried, ranged from $500 to $10,000. The typical trip to the Klondike was by way of steamer up the inside passage of southeastern Alaska to the head of Lynn Canal where the miners were dumped on the tide flats by the steamers and allowed to unload their own goods from ship to scow and scow to wagon. There the miner could shift for himself and choose his route to the interior. The White Pass was about 45 miles long and the Chilkoot about thirty-five. The former was the better advertised but the latter probably the more practical. These passes served as a winnower to separate the hardy stampeder able to stand the rigors of the interior from the weakling, and consequently the average Klondike miner was the healthful, law-abiding type. In the late autumn of '97, 3,700 horses lay dead on the White Pass Trail; it was described as looking like a battlefield. The Chilkoot Pass at one point had a thousand steps cut in the ice. Up this steep ascent the stampeder had to carry his pack of 75 to 200 pounds and "cold-footers," as they were known, had a convenient means of exit always at hand. They had simply to step out from the steps and slide quickly to the base where they could start on the long trail back home. Once at the summit there still remained stormy lakes to cross on boats built with timbers felled in the mountains, and rapids to shoot such as Miles Canyon and the White Horse. A trip of three months from the States to Dawson was considered fairly good time.

Once arriving at Dawson, the stampeder's work was scarcely begun. He was greeted by a veritable street of tents and cabins up and down the small streams along the Klondike River, all of which represented claims already located. He must then seek out his own vacant stream where he could pan out the gravel until he made "a showing." But the great majority of those who started for the Klondike never reached this point. The total figures on the rush are interesting. From 1885 to 1895 the Yukon territory, in which the Klondike was entirely located, produced a million and a quarter in gold. In the year 1897 alone, before the rush

Stampeders packing up the ice steps of Chilkoot Pass.

had reached its height, this sum was trebled. From 1896 to 1904 over $100,000,000 in gold was produced, and the annual yield from '98 to 1904 was never under ten million dollars. Since 1904, the average annual yield has dropped considerably but it is safe to say that the Klondike originally contained well over two hundred million dollars in gold. If we consider that 200,000 people were more or less active stampeders in this rush it is clear that the average income was about $1,000 and the average expense as we have already seen was around $5,000. But this discrepancy is far from telling the truth. A very small percentage of those taking part in the Klondike rush made money. Probably less than one-seventh got any gold at all and a small proportion of that number cleared expenses. This picture is far different from the one that was most usually drawn in the heyday of the rush when men were told of one small claim of eighty-six feet that made $10,000 in two days and returned to its owner a total of close to three-quarters of a million dollars. Many a failure started north with ambitions to emulate the career of Alexander MacDonald who made five million dollars and earned the title "King of the Klondike."

While the Klondike lay entirely in Canada its story properly belongs in Alaskan history, as the Klondike was and is always linked with Alaska in the mind of the layman. Moreover, the thousands of stampeders disappointed in the Klondike spread down the Yukon River and up its tributaries until they had panned out the gravels of much of the interior of Alaska. Indeed, many of those who originally came to the Klondike still remain in Alaska hoping one day to make their big strike. Moreover, the most popular routes to the Klondike were through Alaska. The passes have already been described and White Pass was chosen as the site of a railroad which was open to the summit in the late fall of '99 and which proved more of a gold mine to its owners than many of the claims staked out by its passengers. The tide water terminal of this railroad was the town of Skagway—a typical frontier stampede camp—and as such not without its typical frontier characters.

Probably the most famous of these was "Soapy" Smith, "bad man and bluffer." Jefferson R. Smith was born in Georgia and earned his nickname in the Colorado rush where he worked a swindle game selling soap. There he murdered, gambled, bluffed people at politics and acted the philanthropist as the contingency required, from 1883 to 1891. When invited to leave he wandered to the neighboring camp of Creede and then to Mexico and finally to Seattle to join the Klondike rush in the summer of 1897. He saw his great opportunity in Skagway and remained there to organize his gang that winter. His first opportunity was the old shell game worked half way up White Pass Trail. Here the lowly hand sledder and the lordly pack train would come trudging by to be inveigled at a try for easy money after seeing some of Soapy's confederates beat the game. Soapy collected thousands of dollars without leaving Skagway but this palled on him and he opened gambling houses in the town proper. His most famous venture, "Jeff's Place," was the scene of playing for big stakes, which was considered the thing to do but was also too often the scene of robberies

"Soapy" Smith, Alaskan bad man of Klondike rush.

and even murders. With his five ex-convicts as lieutenants, he gradually enlarged his activities until he was able to bluff the citizens out of lynching one of his henchmen who had shot the deputy marshal. Each success made him bolder until July 6, 1898 he robbed Stewart, a returning miner, of $2,700 by the shell game. This aroused the miners and a mass meeting was held on the end of one of the long docks on July eighth. Frank Reid, a civil engineer, was stationed as a guard at the land end of the dock. When Soapy heard of the meeting he tried to bluff Reid out but the latter stood his ground with drawn pistol. Soapy shot it out with him and both men died, but gang rule was ended at Skagway.

Just as the height of the fever of the Klondike stampede was abating, gold was discovered on Seward Peninsula near Cape Nome. The excitements of '98 were repeated, with all conditions magnified because of the easier access to the new diggings. In 1896, Seward Peninsula, which forms the nearest approach to Asia in Alaska, was a barren waste with a few hundred Esquimaux and a score of whites. Ten years later it had a permanent population of about 4,000 and a summer population of 10,000, with an annual contribution to the world's wealth of eight million dollars. The first mining on the peninsula was at Omalik on Fish River in 1891, where silver was found in small quantities. The telegraph expedition of 1863 had discovered gold in that vicinity and employees of the silver mines made discoveries also. A group of disappointed prospectors, including D. B. Libby, who had been a member of the Western Union Telegraph expedition, returning from Kotzebue Sound in March, 1898, discovered gold in paying quantities near Ophir Creek. A miners' government was immediately set up and a recorder from their number appointed. That summer, working with crude tools, a small group took out between $50,000 and $100,000. However, this aroused very little interest, as Alaskans were becoming satiated with news of new strikes and refused to be as gullible as they had been at first. Gold was discovered at Cape Nome in the latter part of July of '98 and work was started in late September. Although the ground was frozen and conditions were very unfavorable, $1,800 was taken out in the first month of work. This proved to the old timers on the lower Yukon that Nome was a real camp and a small rush from nearby workings resulted in the organization of the Cape Nome mining district in October by forty men. These men abused the territorial laws by staking up over 18,000 acres of available mining land. By the following May there were 250 miners in Nome and by the fall of '99, 3,000.

By this time the world at large had heard of the Nome strikes and the frenzied rush was under way. As most of the land was already located, claim jumping started, with no one to enforce the law except a few soldiers from the government post at St. Michaels. Dissension grew and the miners resorted to their familiar remedy of a "miners' meeting." This was a simple, typically Anglo-Saxon form of preserving order in new camps. A man with a grievance would call a meeting of all the miners in the camp. Before this group he would tell his case and his opponent would state his. Both would have an opportunity to reply and then the group of miners would vote on the merits of the case. The punishments were simple. Theft or threatening with weapons received banishment, murderers were hanged, quarrelsome types were allowed to fight it out. The miners appointed their own recorder who kept a memoranda of all claims located, and the amount of improvement work done annually to comply with the laws. This miners' meeting worked well until the rush to a new camp began, when the horde of newcomers, including undesirables, made the meeting more mob rule than justice.

Civil strife seemed imminent at Nome over the question of claim jumping, when a soldier and John Hummel, a miner seeking a cure for scurvy, discovered gold on the beach almost simultaneously. Nome Beach was one of the typical barrier strands which line the shallow coast of Bering Sea. It stretches along the shore for 25 miles, averaging about two hundred feet in width. This narrow strand soon swarmed with 2,000 miners making $20 to $100 a day, with rockers, pans and all manner of contrivances for extracting gold. In two months, a million dollars was taken from these beach sands. This first excitement resulted in taking the cream of placer gold from the beach, but the idea of gold lying at the ocean's edge was one of the greatest factors in attracting those from the States to this country. The mining on the beach continued to be the poor man's salvation down to as late as the fall of 1907 when one claim gave $40,000 in three days' sluicing.

The winter of '99 and the spring of 1900 was a prosperous one at Nome because all of the residents were inured to

Alaskan hardships and all were prosperous with the result of their beach diggings. The spring brought the motliest crew that has ever assembled in an Alaskan mining camp. Fed by advertisements and stock sales which stressed easy money, men and women came from all parts of the United States, each with a clever idea as to how they were to make a fortune in a few days. Their ideas ranged all the way from the rental of latrines to mining machines designed to roll out into the ocean and extract the gold that was supposed to exist there by submarine sluicing. Here there was no Chilkoot Pass to separate the chaff from the wheat and people utterly unfit for Alaskan conditions were dumped on the Nome Beach by lighters from the ships riding far out at sea. By August 1, 162 steamships and 70 sailing vessels had landed 18,000 people. Many of these returned as soon as possible after seeing how bitterly they had been disappointed. Many others stayed to eke out a miserable existence for a year, not caring to leave the town of Nome and go into the surrounding hills which were still rich with undiscovered minerals. Prices mounted sky high. Two to three dollars was paid for a bunk or a meal. Eggs cost a dollar apiece. As usual with such excitements those clever enough to leave mining to the others and devote themselves to catering to the needs of the stampeders made comfortable incomes. Rex Beach was one of the thousands who landed in the rush and has since boasted that he was one of the few college men who was able to pay his way back to the States. This rush ranks high in gold production with the other great excitements of the nineteenth century. California in its greatest years—1851-

Nome Beach at height of gold rush.

Bringing in the mail at Nome. Lightering was necessary for all transportation to and from vessels.

1853—produced $62,000,000. The Klondike in the two years —1898-1900—produced $40,000,000, and from 1896-1906, $118,725,000. Seward Peninsula in 1899-1900 produced $7,500,000, and from 1898 to 1906, $37,247,000. Geologists estimated the gold area of the Seward Peninsula as great as that of California, but the rate of working less rapid, as the climate and water power were not so favorable. The Klondike has one-tenth the area of these other two districts and since 1906 has showed signs of exhaustion.

The riffraff that congregated at Nome made the need for strict law and order imperative from the first. Unfortunately, Nome, which needed such conditions most, lacked them most. The military under General Randall had ruled the country as well as they were able until Federal Judge Arthur H. Noyes of Minnesota and Dakota arrived. Men breathed a sigh of relief, thinking they were now to have civil law instead of martial law, but they quickly saw that the change had been to judicial corruption rather than civil government. Alexander McKenzie came to Nome on the same ship with Judge Noyes. He represented the Alaskan Gold Mining Company, a New York corporation in which he was reputedly the biggest stockholder. His chief assets became the rich claims on Anvil Creek which his men jumped from the Wild Goose and Pioneer Mining Companies. Four days after their arrival, the Judge and his henchmen had collaborated, with the result that McKenzie had been appointed receiver of four of the richest claims in the district. All this was done before court was officially organized and on the flimsiest of pretexts without legal precedent or procedure. McKenzie's bond was fixed at $5,000, although one of the claims yielded $15,000 a day. Under his receivership he could work the mine and hold the gold subject to the order of Judge Noyes. The Judge refused to hear appeals and would brook no interference.

Faced with such a combination the Wild Goose Company sent secret messengers to San Francisco to get writs to stop this high-handed judicial robbery. Meanwhile, wholesale receiverships granted to McKenzie or his aides frightened all legitimate miners into stopping operations before they disclosed gold in sufficient quantity to attract the cupidity of these robbers. On September 14, the writs arrived but the Judge and McKenzie refused to heed them. Fights were narrowly avoided and additional messengers were sent to San Francisco to get power to arrest McKenzie for contempt of court. McKenzie was seized and taken to California just before Bering Sea froze for the winter. After a long legal fight there, he was sentenced to a year in jail in February, 1901. The court in its judgment said it was "a shocking record with no parallel in the jurisprudence of this country." McKenzie was pardoned under suspicious circumstances by the President after only three months of his sentence had been served. Judge Noyes with his district attorney and other officials were called for trial in October, 1901. Noyes left Nome two months earlier to prepare his case and provided a fitting culmination to his career by granting last minute orders and injunctions which gave extra-legal privileges to his friends, who came out to his boat to see him. He was found guilty by the Court of Appeals and fined $1,000; his assistants were given from four to twelve months each. In February, 1902, he was removed from office and Judge Wickersham succeeded him. He was to bring law and order for the first time to Nome.

These rushes gave a tremendous impetus to Alaska in general and to the population especially. This sudden growth was for the most part unhealthy, as are all booms. All censuses before 1900 were more in the nature of estimates than accurate counts of the total population, as transportation facilities made accuracy impossible. In 1867, it had been estimated that there were about 30,000 people in Alaska, of whom only 3,000 were civilized. Since that time there had been a fairly steady influx of Americans, chiefly prospectors. The first attempt at an accurate census was made in 1880 by Ivan Petroff, who made an extensive personal tour of the country and based his survey on this tour, combined with ten years close touch with Alaska, and the work of his agents. He based his census largely on the records of the Russian Church and his work has been called by some "a mere estimate"; it was necessarily faulty. For example, his southeastern Alaska agent made little effort to secure a count at Juneau where the rush was in progress, and his work was so poor that his pay was refused. Nevertheless, Petroff's figures probably represent a good minimum. He gives the total population as 33,426, of which 430 were whites. The census of 1890 shows practically the same total population but an increase of the white population to over 6,000. The 1900 census, which was taken in the summer and included the Nome Beach stampeders, showed a total of 34,000 whites which, with a fairly fixed Indian total of 30,000, gave Alaska 64,000 people as a maximum.

For such a population, Congress was still legislating as it had in 1867 or 1884. The governors, appointed under the Organic Act of '84, annually reported the growing needs of Alaska as: first, land laws, so that permanent settlers would be encouraged to own land which they could protect legally; second, the abolition of prohibition, which was harder to enforce than all other laws combined; third, representation in Congress; fourth, larger powers for Alaskan officers; fifth, more intelligent laws; and finally, proper regulation of resources. While these half dozen ills were annually brought to the notice of Congress in the strongest language possible by each successive governor, Congress steadily refused to take note of them. The greatest evil was prohibition and this was finally repealed in 1899 for a strict license law. The Act of 1884 had provided for the use of the Oregon laws in Alaska, wherever they did not conflict with the laws of the United States or the Act of 1884. Such an anomalous arrangement made court procedure always uncertain. Each successive judge had to reconcile the three codes and his successor usually differed with his interpretation. The provision for juries was almost impossible to enforce and the system of making commissioners and deputy commissioners dependent for salaries on the fees they received from cases they handled was pernicious in every way. After repeated complaints and the prominence given Alaska by the "rush era," a commission was appointed by the President which reported a code of criminal law and procedure in 1898, but here again Congress was remiss and did not approve its work until the spring of '99. A civil code was adopted in 1900 providing for three judicial districts and forming the basis of the Alaskan judicial system to-day. Alaska's ills then, as now, were lack of central power in the government at Washington, lack of scientific knowledge as to Alaska's conditions, lack of personal and public interest in Alaska, and finally the use of Alaskan offices as political patronage. Transportation facilities were practically impossible—so much so that several governors never went outside of southeastern Alaska during their term of office and none visited the interior of Alaska in the first decade after 1884. Under such conditions Alaska played host to the greatest horde of adventurous spirits assembled anywhere in North America. That there was so little lawlessness and crime is a credit to the members of the Anglo-Saxon race.

CHAPTER VIII

INTERNATIONAL COMPLICATIONS

THE "rush" era brought Alaska on the international stage socially and economically. Two disputes with other countries over her boundary lines and seal fisheries at about the same time brought the country to the fore politically, so that Alaska might well be called a topic of the day in the decade from 1895 to 1905. The ambitious pretensions of Russia in the Czar's ukase of 1821 had, as we have seen, brought protests from the United States and England, which resulted in the treaties of 1824 and 1825. At that time both countries sought primarily from Russia renunciation of her claims to all of the Pacific Coast north of 51° and 100 miles off shore. They disputed these claims chiefly in order to maintain their commercial advantages in that region. The United States treaty of 1824 secured no more than this with a limitation of Russia to 54° 40′. The English treaty of 1825, however, went farther and defined the eastern Alaskan boundary as follows:

III. The line of demarcation between the possessions of the High Contracting Parties upon the coast of the continent and the islands of America to the Northwest, shall be drawn in the following manner:

Commencing from the southernmost point of the island called Prince of Wales Island which point lies in the parallel of 54 degrees 40 minutes north latitude, and between the 131st and 132d degree of west longitude, the said line shall ascend to the north along the channel called Portland Channel as far as the point of the continent where it strikes the 56th degree of north latitude; from this last-mentioned point, the line of demarcation shall follow the summit of the mountains situated parallel to the coast, as far as the point of intersection of the 141st degree of west longitude; and finally, from the said point of intersection, the said meridian line of the 141st degree, in its prolongation as far as the Frozen Ocean, shall form the limit between the Russian and British Possessions on the Continent of America to the northwest.

IV. With reference to the line of demarcation laid down in the preceding article, it is understood:

First. That the island called Prince of Wales Island shall belong wholly to Russia.

Second. That wherever the summit of the mountains which extend in a direction parallel to the coast from the 56th degree of north latitude to the point of intersection of the 141st degree of west longitude shall prove to be at the distance of more than ten marine leagues from the ocean, the limit between the British Possessions and the line of the coast (la lisiere de cote) which is to belong to Russia, as above mentioned, shall be formed by a line parallel to the windings (sinuosites) of the coast, and which shall never exceed the distance of ten marine leagues therefrom.

The treaty of 1867 by which Alaska was transferred to the United States referred to the line of 1825 as the proper boundary between that country and Canada. Practically from the acquisition of Alaska both England and the United States had urged more definite location of this boundary. President Grant had suggested a settlement of the line in 1872, and Canada made urgent and almost yearly requests from that time on. It was felt that early settlement of the question, while the country involved still remained comparatively young and little used, would avoid future complications, but definite action could not be obtained.[1] The first agreement of the two countries in 1892 resulted in a joint survey which fixed the northern portion of the line from Mt. St. Elias along the 141st meridian to the Arctic Ocean. Up to this time there had been no actual dispute but questions had been raised in connection with the Cassiar gold excitement of 1873 and other discoveries in 1877. However, the Klondike rush of '98 made Canada exceedingly anxious to secure a port of entry near the Yukon fields at the head of Lynn Canal. For the first time Canada now laid claim to the ports of Dyea and Skagway. The dispute was referred to an Anglo-American Joint High Commission, to be taken up with several other points of difference between the two countries. But the United States refused to accept arbitration of this question. Proponents of the Canadian side of the dispute pointed out what they considered the inconsistency of the position taken by the United States. They reminded Americans that the United States had just previously forced arbitration of the Venezuelan boundary question on England. However, the circumstances of the latter dispute were not the same. A modus vivendi was agreed upon in the fall of 1899, in which the United States made concessions to Canada but specifically provided that these would not prejudice the claims of either party in the ultimate settlement.

The points in dispute related entirely to the line from Prince of Wales Island to Mt. St. Elias. The treaty of 1825

[1] J. B. Moore, North American Review, October 1899, also T. Hodgins' "Alaska Canadian Boundary."

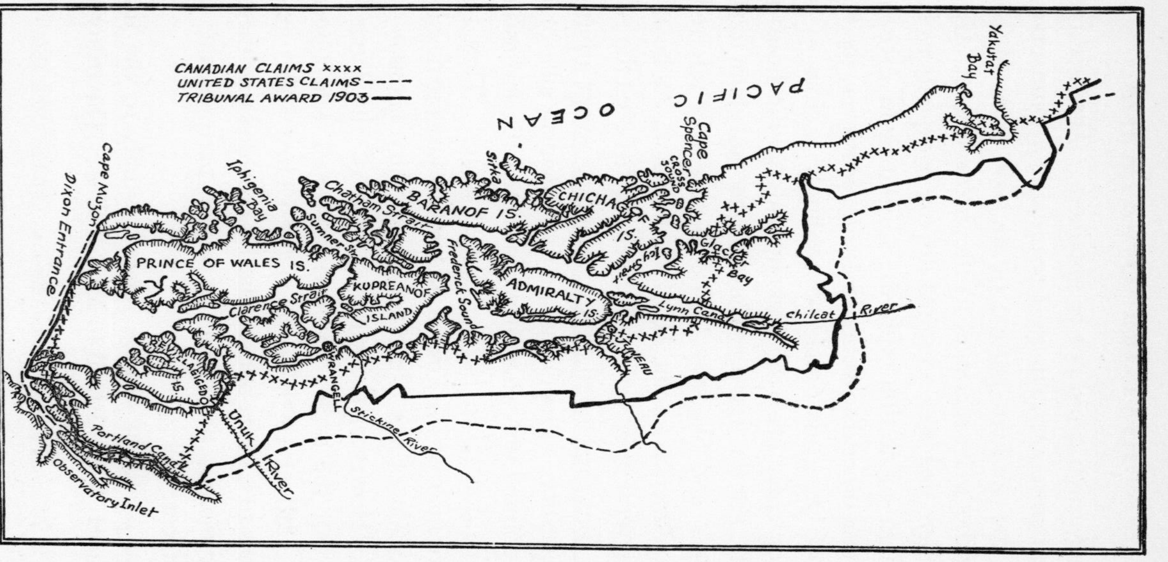
CANADIAN CLAIMS xxxx
UNITED STATES CLAIMS ----
TRIBUNAL AWARD 1903
PACIFIC OCEAN
Yakutat Bay
Cape Spencer
CROSS SOUND
Glacier Bay
Icy Strait
Chilcat River
Lynn Canal
JUNEAU
CHICHAGOF IS.
ADMIRALTY IS.
Sitka
BARANOF IS.
Frederick Sound
Chatham Strait
KUPREANOF ISLAND
Sumner Str.
WRANGELL
Stickine River
Iphigenia Bay
PRINCE OF WALES IS.
Clarence Strait
REVILLAGIGEDO IS.
Unuk River
Portland Canal
Observatory Inlet
Cape Muzon
Dixon Entrance

had failed to account for the fact that the Portland Canal lay about fifty miles due east of the southern point of Prince of Wales Island. The Canadians claimed that inasmuch as the treaty did not provide for going east this distance, the "Portland Channel" referred to in the treaty really meant the present Clarence Strait. Further than this, the proviso for the line running ten leagues from the sea did not make it clear as to whether this distance should be measured from the head of inlets; or should be measured from the general coast line and thereby go across the mouths of the inlets; or should be measured from the outer fringe of the islands skirting the mainland. Finally, further explorations of the territory showed that it was practically impossible to fix on the mountains referred to in the treaty as "parallel to the coast."

A treaty was drawn providing for an arbitral tribunal to meet in the fall of 1903 which would give the dispute judicial consideration. The United States nominees were Secretary of State Elihu Root, Senator Henry Cabot Lodge of Massachusetts and former Senator George Turner of Washington. Canada objected to these officials as being non-judicial and already prejudiced to the United States case. However, England did not see fit to sustain these objections. The Canadian judges were Mr. A. B. Aylesworth of Toronto and Sir Louis Jette, Lieutenant Governor of Quebec. Baron Alverstone, Lord Chief Justice of England, acted as the third English judge, and as chairman of the tribunal. Canada felt that Lord Alverstone was the only impartial representative and hence that she could not hope to secure better than a tie vote and would probably receive a 4 to 2 defeat on most points, which proved to be the case. The two Canadian members refused to sign the decision. The trial was public, which helped give justice to the decision but the decision itself was secret. The decision was more in the nature of a diplomatic compromise than an arbitration of the points at issue. England and Canada dropped their claim of Clarence Strait being "Portland Channel," although they pointed out that it would be easier to confuse the name of a body of water than a compass direction, and hence that there was more ground for believing that Clarence Strait might have been the "Portland Channel" of Vancouver's discovery than that the treaty said north and meant east. It was decided that the boundary line should run ten leagues from the sea and also should run around all deep inlets. In other words, that Canada would not secure a Pacific port north of 54° 40′. This decision destroyed Canada's hope for a port at the head of Lynn Canal.

The tribunal did not attempt to fix upon the mountains parallel to the coast but contented themselves with adopting a compromise line between the Canadian claim of the peaks nearest the coast and the United States claim farther inland. Having once determined that the southern boundary should run east to the present Portland Canal, the difficulty arose as to what constituted the proper entrance to the Canal—that is, whether the boundary should run north of the four islands at the mouth of the Canal, as Canada claimed, or south of these islands. These islands in themselves were then and have been since uninhabited, but they were considered of great strategic value because they controlled the entrance to

Port Simpson harbor, the contemplated terminus for a Trans-Canadian Railroad. The tribunal compromised illogically here by giving the United States the first two small islands and awarding Canada the larger Pierce and Wales Islands in the Canal. Canada has since located the terminus of the railroad farther south at Prince Rupert in a harbor controlled completely by Canadian territory. This decision, although extremely favorable to the United States, aroused some opposition because of the loss of the two islands on the southern boundary, and because it was felt that the eastern boundary approached too near the coast at several places, notably the Stikine River and Glacier Bay.

In regard to Glacier Bay, the boundary was originally measured twelve miles inland from the east front of the glaciers of 1894 so as to get a direct line to Mt. Fairweather. By August 1, 1912, the glaciers had receded so that Canada had a harbor at this point. The only difficulty is that the harbor lies in the midst of a snowy desert and cannot be reached except by way of American waters. It is probable that Canada will lose this harbor in the future when the glaciers fill again, but at the present time she is breaking the spirit of the treaty award, which was to block off Canada from any port in the Pacific north of 54° 40′. Glaciers in the Mt. St. Elias region are moving backward and forward similarly, alternately giving us territory and taking it away from us. No economic or political significance seems to attach to this interesting feature, but the lesson contained is that boundaries should not be located with reference to glaciers. Another interesting feature of the boundary dispute is that in 1908, Leo Nebokoff found, among some old Russian documents in the archives at Sitka, an order from the Russian Government to the Governor of Alaska to bury tablets, bearing the Russian coat of arms, at different points along the Alaskan coast so as to insure her claims to that territory. Some of these tablets have been located as far south as British Columbia and had these discoveries been made prior to 1903, it is possible that the United States might have laid claim to the whole of the Pacific Coast, thereby barring Canada from a Pacific port. However, Canada does not recognize that she was fortunate in receiving as favorable consideration as she did in the boundary award, and her legislators have repeatedly urged that she bring pressure to bear upon the United States to grant to her the "panhandle" of Alaska, as the southeastern portion is known. Such motions have been presented in the Canadian Parliament as recently as 1927. Canada feels that this panhandle acts as a barrier and is detrimental to the development of the northern part of British Columbia. The United States has given Canada all the consideration possible, based on historical grounds. Any further concessions would be unwarranted.

The second international dispute and perhaps the more important because of its long standing and the amounts and principles involved was the Bering Sea controversy over the fur seal fisheries. This dispute in a sense also arises from boundary complications, as the treaty of 1867 gives to the United States all territory east of a line drawn from Bering Strait to a point midway between the Commander Islands and Attu, the furthermost Aleutian Island. The early American contention that Bering Sea was a "mare clausum" was based in part upon this treaty which inferred a territorial right over the portion of Bering Sea beyond the three-mile limit to the boundary.

The fur seal, which has proved especially valuable to mankind, was originally divided into three great herds, which made their homes on Robin Island in the Sea of Okhotsk, on the Commander Islands, and the largest herd on the Pribilof Islands in Bering Sea. The herd would arrive on the islands of St. Paul and St. George in June, where the old males would each gather a harem around themselves and force the young bachelor seals to congregate alone. Here the mating would be done and the pups raised until early fall, each female bearing one pup. The herd then left the Pribilofs to make their way rapidly down the Pacific Ocean about as far south as San Francisco, where they circled about and made their way leisurely up the American coast back to the islands. From the discovery of the islands in 1787, Russia had recognized the tremendous value of these fisheries and had early given a private company a monopoly over their breeding grounds. This company in its early days killed off the males and females without discrimination, but such a policy soon defeated itself by decreasing the herd so rapidly that the kill was later restricted to the bachelor seals who were driven to a point inland on the islands and there clubbed to death. By this method a large kill could be made each year without hindering the growth of the herd in any way. This policy of granting a monopoly to a private company was continued by our government after the purchase of 1867. The Alaska Commercial Company and later the Northern Commercial Company held exclusive control over the islands and over the kill throughout this period. The Alaska Commercial Company paid the government $55,000 a year and a percentage on each skin taken. In the early years they took 100,000 skins a year. The market price in 1868 was $2.50 per skin. This gradually increased as the skins became fashionable, until it was $30.00 a skin in 1890. The increase in value of the skins and the tremendous profits being made by private companies brought on increased pelagic fishing.

Pelagic or open sea killing of seals had been practiced from earliest times by the Pacific Coast Indians. These natives would put out from shore in their canoes at about the time that the herd swimming leisurely north approached the latitude of their villages, and would spear the seals while they were sleeping on the surface of the water. As long as it was kept under such conditions, pelagic sealing was no serious problem. The total catch from 1868 to 1878 was probably not over 5,000 skins a year, but the increased demand for seal skins brought on vessels which could go out to sea with a load of canoes and follow the herd day by day on their northern journey. By this method the Indians were supplied with a convenient haven for the canoes to return at night with the kill of the day. In 1878 there was one vessel so engaged. By 1892 there were one hundred and twenty-two such vessels, each with from five to twenty canoes. In 1894, ninety-five vessels took 140,000 skins.

Our government had protested against this pelagic fishing from the first. The protest of 1881 set forth the far-fetched American claim that Bering Sea east of the Russian boundary was all under the exclusive jurisdiction of the United States and that the three-mile limit did not exist there. Government officials acting on this interpretation in 1886 seized three Canadian vessels engaged in pelagic fishing in Bering Sea; five more were seized in the following year. England justifiably protested against such high-handed actions. But at the same time, her statesmen followed the selfish policy of Canada in refusing to agree to any sensible plan for international protection of the herd. As our seizures continued, relations with England became strained and pressure on the United States for more seizures grew as the land kill decreased from the early figure of 100,000 a year to 20,000 a year. An arbitration treaty was agreed upon in 1892, whereby a board met in Paris in 1893 made up of two representatives from the United States, two from England and one each from France, Italy and Sweden. Their decision of August 15, 1893, favored England in theory and the United States in practice. They decided that under the principles of international law previous American seizures were illegal. With relation to the seals, they, first, prohibited all pelagic fishing within a sixty-mile circle around the Pribilof Islands. Secondly, they established a closed season for fur seals in May, June and July over all Bering Sea and the Pacific Ocean north of 35°. Finally, they prohibited the use of nets, firearms and explosives in taking seals, and made other regulations as to proper licensing of vessels and similar matters.

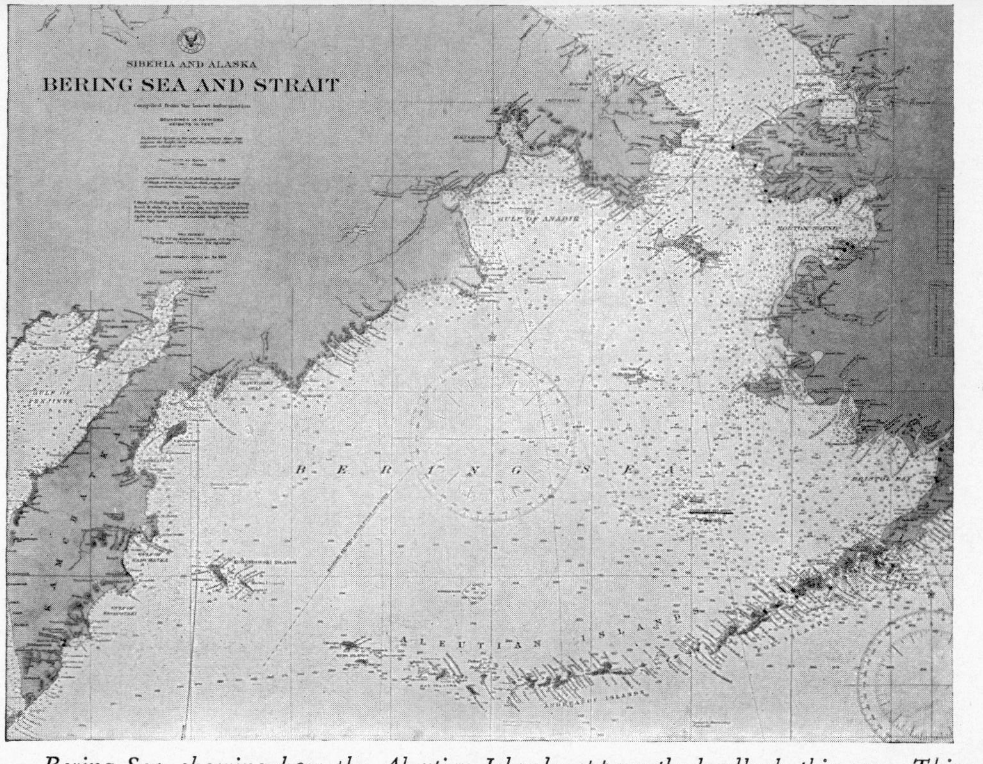

Bering Sea, showing how the Aleutian Islands apparently landlock this sea. This gave rise to the "Mare Clausum" claim of the United States. In reality many of the islands are nearly one hundred miles apart. (The Pribilof Islands are shown underlined east of Bristol Bay.)

This Paris award denied the United States claim that Bering Sea was a "mare clausum" and consequently denied the justice of our seizures. It, however, only partially recognized the evil of pelagic sealing. Our scientists had declared that such sealing was invidious in that killing at sea did not discriminate between males and females and that consequently seventy-five to eighty per cent of the seals so killed were females and that ten per cent of all seals killed were lost through sinking. On the other hand, they pointed out that the land kill, of bachelor seals only, did not permanently hurt the herd in any way whatsoever. It was felt that the Paris award did not provide properly against this destructive process and both England and America admitted that it was not a settlement of the problem. However, the award averted war and gave the seals some protection; it had cleared all doubtful points of international law, and with the scientific investigations of 1898 on the islands pointed clearly to pelagic fishing as the sole evil to be corrected. The herd did not prosper under these half-way conditions and the controversy was further embittered by a Japanese seal raid on the islands in the summer of 1906.[1] It is interesting to note that this raid was supposed to have been conducted by Abe McLean, the sea wolf of Jack London's fiction, who had performed similar raids ten years before under the Mexican flag. The United States felt that such an act was absolute robbery or piracy and that a treaty should be negotiated to stop a recurrence of such things. The whole problem was settled by the North Pacific Sealing Convention on July 7,

[1] Twelve of the raiders were captured and five killed.

1911, whereby pelagic fishing was prohibited and all countries bordering on Bering Sea engaged to protect this resource. This convention is still in force and effect although Japan is seeking a conference for alteration of some phases of it.

Alaska and the United States were indeed fortunate in gaining favorable decisions in these two great international disputes. While the imperialism and bravado of President Roosevelt and his government almost brought on war in regard to them at various stages in their negotiation, the good sense of both countries brought about settlements that have left little or no rancor. This result can in large part be laid to the willingness of England to gain coöperation with the United States so as to have her as an ally in world politics. Canadian public opinion has sometimes felt that England was over-tractable in these disputes because Canadian rather than English interests were at stake and they have felt that England deserted them at critical stages. However, the perspective of two decades seems to show that both disputes were settled in about as fair a manner as could have been found.

CHAPTER IX

TERRITORIAL GOVERNMENT

THE United States had acquired Alaska while still busy settling her own western territory. Consequently, through too great occupation nearer home, and the usual ignorance that a republic has of colonial government, Alaska suffered for the first thirty years of American rule. The gold rush of 1898 made the problem of Alaskan government so much greater, and so much more pressing than that of any other dependency that American colonial policy was only beginning to catch up with the problem at the outbreak of the World War.

Every governor from 1884 to 1899 urged a criminal and civil code for Alaska. Finally, the influx of thousands of miners to the country in the last years of the century forced Congress to appoint a commission which provided a code of criminal and civil procedure for the district, together with a high liquor license law, additional judicial divisions and additional commissioners. In 1909 the fourth judicial division was added. This system is one of federal courts but the courts are answerable to Congress and the judges are subject to the authority of the President. The system has fallen far short of solving Alaska's problem of law and order—so much so that Governor Riggs in his report of 1919 cited as a "crying need" police protection outside of the towns.

To-day there are less than one hundred officers to enforce the law for 600,000 square miles of territory.

Congressional attention once turned to Alaska continued to provide sadly-needed government. Towns were given the right to incorporate and Alaskans, for the first time, were able to live under civil jurisdiction corresponding in some slight respect to that of their fellow citizens in the States. Much of this statutory reform was weakened, if not nullified, by the character of Alaskan officialdom in the period. Matthew S. Quay, political boss of Pennsylvania,[1] used the territory as a hunting ground, or better, a dumping ground, for his minions in the East, and many other harassed legislators sent their most importunate office-seekers off to this virgin country.

Her governors were, for the most part, honest though not exceedingly able or outstanding as statesmen. They were prone to look upon their jobs as being primarily to please Washington, and, secondly, to govern Alaska. The first governor, John Kinkead, a former governor of Nevada and merchant of Sitka, was probably above the average. Governor Swineford, the newspaper publisher, attracted attention to Alaska by his vigorous policies but at the same time created personal antagonisms; and Governor Sheakley was below average. Governor John G. Brady, a protégé of the Presbyterian Church, went to Alaska as a missionary in 1878, was appointed Governor in 1897 and held office until 1906, when he was ousted by Roosevelt for unfortunate connections[2]

[1] Capt. Ivy of Philadelphia, Collector of Port 1888-90, Quay man, made millions up there.

[2] J. P. Nichols—Constitutional History of Alaska, p. 271.

with promoters. It is unfortunate that Governor Brady left office under such unfavorable circumstances as he handled his arduous duties through the Klondike and Nome stampedes in a very acceptable manner. His bosom friend and co-worker, Sheldon Jackson, long head of the Presbyterian missions in Alaska, and responsible for the introduction of the reindeer, lost office at the same time. This marked the end of hierarchy rule in Alaska by the Presbyterians. Their influence had been second only to that of the commercial companies. They did valuable work for the Indians, but the whites would no doubt have been better governed if lay interests had held the prestige accorded that church among lobbyists at Washington. Their going marked the advent of politics.

Alaskan legislation in general was hindered by the fact that after 1898 she was grouped with our other dependencies, and she suffered from the connection. Porto Rico, Hawaii and the Philippines all received official representation at Washington before her; yet the revenue of Alaska continued to outstrip that of all the other dependencies. High license taxes on liquors were levied in 1900, and the Alaskans were justified in objecting to them as taxation without representation. The outstanding legislative relief of the period was that the vexing and neglected question of lands was partially settled by the Homestead laws of 1903. The inability of Alaskans to secure legal title to their lands was one of the greatest retarding factors in the history of the country and had been agitated more than any other single thing by the governors and the official representatives. Curiously enough the Organic Law of 1884 specifically forbade the application of American land laws to the territory. The relief in 1903 came so late that its true effects cannot be ascertained even to-day.

For forty-five years Alaska had no legislature except Congress and for thirty-nine years she had no representation in the aforesaid Congress. All this despite the fact that the question was vigorously debated in every Congress from the Fifty-third to the Fifty-ninth inclusive. Finally, through the recommendation of President Roosevelt, the election of a delegate by Alaskans to coöperate with the government at Washington was authorized. This delegate was given a seat in the House of Representatives and was admitted to all the prerogatives of a Congressman except the right to vote. His powers were less than those of the representatives of our tropical dependencies. After two short terms by Delegate Waskey and Delegate Cale, Judge James Wickersham of Fairbanks was elected to the office, which he held for a number of years, and through which he secured much beneficial legislation for Alaska. Wickersham and later Sutherland held the office long enough to make their personal knowledge of Alaska of value to the powers in Washington and thereby aided their constituents.

A local legislature had been urged in the earliest governors' reports and many bills to that effect were introduced in Congress. The opposition was strong because many felt that the country was too sparsely populated to bear the expense of a territorial legislature. When the Territorial Act, or the so-called "Home Rule Bill" was passed in the fall of 1912, Alaska had a denser population per square mile than any other territory of the United States, except Montana, when granted an assembly. The act was patterned after the Washington Territorial Act of 1853. By the bill Alaska was given a Senate of eight and a House of sixteen to be chosen equally from each of the four judicial districts. There is no real reason why this legislature should not have been unicameral except the tradition that all American assemblies are divided into two bodies. The members are elected from the same constituencies, have the same qualifications and perform largely the same functions. The powers of the legislature are limited in many respects as shown by the following wording of the Act:

> The legislative power of the Territory shall extend to all rightful subjects of legislation not inconsistent with the Constitution and laws of the United States. It may not pass any law interfering with the primary disposal of the soil; it may not levy taxes that are not uniform upon the same class of subjects; it may not grant any exclusive or special privileges without the affirmative approval of Congress; it may not legalize lotteries or gambling; it may make no provision respecting the manufacture or sale of spiritous or intoxicating liquors; it may not authorize bonded indebtedness or the creation of any debt by the Territory or municipalities thereof; it may not appropriate any public money for the benefit of any sectarian or denominational school, or any school not under the exclusive control of the Government; it may not authorize the extension of the credit of the Government of the Territory, or any subdivision thereof, to any incorporated company; it may not create or assume any indebtedness for the actual running expenses of the Territorial Government in excess of the actual income of the Territory for a given year; it may not levy any tax for Territorial purposes in excess of one per centum upon the assessed valuation of property, nor within the incorporated towns in excess of two per

centum; it may not pass any law providing for the formation of county government within the Territory without the affirmative approval of Congress; it may not "alter, amend, modify or repeal" the "game" and "fish" laws passed by Congress and in force in Alaska. . . ." It simply may not change the laws of Congress already in force relating to these subjects, but the act has a proviso to the effect that "This provision shall not operate to prevent the legislature from imposing other and additional taxes or licenses." . . . It may alter, amend, or repeal any part of the Alaska Codes, both civil and criminal; it may impose road and poll taxes; it may legislate upon such subjects as quarantine, sanitation, public health, supervision of banks, registration of births, marriages and deaths, compulsory school attendance, relief of destitution, insurance, regulation of manufacturing, mining and other industrial corporations, and generally for the purpose of protecting the civil and religious liberties of the citizen.

In short, the legislature is really nothing more than the agent of Congress with certain limited powers to be exercised as long as Congress may allow. Congress may repeal any act of the legislature, even the legislature itself. As indicated above, legislative powers were given to Alaska making the territory complete in every sense of the word at a very late date in its history. In 1912, Alaska had a greater population than nine states had when admitted to the Union. For example, Nevada had 42,000 when admitted to statehood, Ohio, 45,000, Oregon 52,000 and Wyoming 60,000 as compared with Alaska's 64,000. Early legislators in Alaska were able, qualified men—not drawn from the professional politician class. As might be expected in a pioneer country, the legislature soon became radical and instead of devoting itself to the immediate problems of the new country, which were many and difficult of solution, it took up the major problems of government and acted upon woman suffrage, prohibition, preferential voting, old age pensions, income tax, territorial official flower, and similar national, sociological, or theoretical questions even before the parent country saw fit to take legislative action in regard to them. The legislature keeps fairly busy, averaging about thirty bills for each two month session. In 1915, it enfranchised Alaskan natives under strict conditions which were made so by the insistence of the Indians themselves. This adds a fairly easily influenced group to the electorate and will not conduce to conservative legislation. The Territorial Act, creating a legislature, went a long way toward answering many of the governmental problems of Alaska. The chief one now remaining is that of administration. At the present time, Alaska is still administered by more than thirty bureaus in Washington operating under every department of the Cabinet. Such a maze of control produces many absurdities and, worse, clogs the wheels of progress. The solution of this problem lies in the future and its recognition of late gives promise that Alaska will be freed from this rule of red tape.

The political education of Alaskans far outstripped Congressional recognition. The conventions of the eighties and nineties were repeated in 1905. This last convention memorialized Congress for relief from specific and general ills and sent three representatives to Washington, but by and large their efforts bore little fruit. The rallying cry of the pioneers from 1900 down to recent times has been that of anti-capitalism, or more specifically "anti-Guggenheimism,"

FEDERAL GOVERNMENT OF

ALASKA

SHOWING CONTROL BY BUREAUS

Topographical Survey	
Geological Survey	
Water Supply	
Maps	
Topographic Survey	NF.
Water Supply	NF.
Government Railroad	
Townsites on "	
Forest Reserves "	
Coal Mines "	
National Monuments	
National Parks	
Weather Stations	
Mineral Lands	NF.
Timber	NF.
Townsites	NF.
Townsites Govt. R.R.	NF.
Trade & Mfg. Sites	NF.
Soldiers Add. Home'd	NF.
Coal Leases	NF.
Oil Leases	NF.
Springs Hot & Min.	NF.
Cemeteries	NF.
Indian Allotments	NF.
Church and School Sites	NF.
Wharf Sites	NF.
Eighty Rod Shore Sp.	NF.
Rights of Way	NF.
Subdivisional Surveys	NF.
Forest Listing Survey	NF.
Agricultural Lands	NF.
Mission Sites	NF.
Roads	NF.
Timber Sales	NF.
Timber Survey	NF.
Fox Farming Leases	NF.
Modnak Island Res.	NF.
Free Use Permits	NF.
Homesteads	NF.
Furseal Fisheries	
Furbearing Animals	
Fur Farming	
Special Fishery Work	
Fixed Fishing Appliance	
Fish Reserves	
Fish Cultural Station	
Coast Surveys	
Lighthouse Reserve	
Inspection Boilers & Hull	
Mariners Licenses	
Station Reserves	
Rights of Way	
Commercial Cable Service	
Commercial Teleg. Service	
Commercial Wireless "	
Unused Govt. Property	
Public Health & Quarant'e	
Immigration Service	
Public Mail Service	
Postal Routes	
Post Offices	
Foreign Consuls	
Joint Rail & Water Rates	
Railroad Rates	

SECRETARY OF INTERIOR
- Governor of Alaska
- Geological Survey
- General Land Office
- Alaska Engineering Comm.
- Bureau of Mines
- National Park Service
- Bureau of Education

SECTY. OF AGRICULTURE
- Bureau of Animal Industry
- Weather Bureau
- Bureau of Public Roads
- Biological Survey
- States Relations
- Forest Service

SECRETARY OF COMMERCE
- Bureau of Fisheries
- Coast & Geodetic Survey
- Lighthouse Service
- Steamboat Inspection
- Bureau of Navigation

SECRETARY OF WAR
- Adjutant General
- Engineer Corps
- Alaska Road Commission
- Signal Corps

SECRETARY OF NAVY
- Bureau of Operations
- Naval Radio

SECRETARY OF TREASURY
- Coast Guard Service
- Customs Service
- Supervising Architect
- Comptroller of Currency
- Public Health

ATTORNEY GENERAL

SECRETARY OF LABOR
- Immigration Bureau

POSTMASTER GENERAL

SECRETARY OF STATE
- Boundary Commission

FEDERAL POWER COMM.

SHIPPING BOARD

INTERST. COMMERCE COMM.

- Historical Museum
- Insane of Alaska
- Game
- School Lands
- Supp. Liquor Traffic
- Agricultural Lands
- Mineral Lands
- Timber Lands
- Townsites - Govt.
- Townsites
- Trade & Manfg. Sites
- Soldiers Homestead
- Coal Land Leases
- Oil Land Leases
- Springs Hot & Mineral
- Cemeteries
- Indian Allotments
- Church and School Sites
- Wharf Sites
- Eighty Rod Shore Sp.
- Rights of Way
- Subdivisional Surveys
- Forest Listing Surveys
- True Homestead
- Mission Sites
- Federal Mine Inspection
- Mine Experiment Station
- Coal Reserves
- Natives
- Native Reserves
- Native Schools
- Native Homesteads
- School Reserves
- Reindeer
- Reindeer Hunting
- School
- Annette Island Reserve
- Bear Family
- Mammals
- Migratory Birds
- Patent Reserves
- Aleutian
- Game Reserves
- Agriculture
- Aids to Navigation
- Army Posts
- River & Harbor Imp.
- Naval Patrol
- Radio Stations
- Revenue Cutter Reserve
- Coast Guard Patrol
- Customs Collection
- Ships Registry
- Public Buildings
- Supervision Nat'n Banks
- Courts
- Public Records
- Boundary Survey
- Water Power
- Steamship Rates

NOTE: No cross reference is made to school, telegraph or other minor reserves where they conflict with major reserves. The total number of reserves in Alaska is 315.

as that famous family had $50,000,000 invested in Alaska by 1908, and, along with this, went opposition to the policy of conservation. The Government attempted to enforce a coal monopoly against bitter opposition, but their efforts were doomed to failure from the beginning because of the lack of proper surveys. Finally, in 1906, the President withdrew all coal lands from private control to stop the growing graft. This action fused the fight against big corporations with that for home rule. Alaskan disgust for Washington, D. C. was intensified by Governor Hoggat, Brady's successor, who made rash and foolish statements that the interior could never hope to be any more than a temporary residence for placer miners, and characterized Alaskan agriculture as a "moonshine" industry.

The campaign of 1908 for a delegate was a bitter one, with James Wickersham winning and starting his long career in the office. The succeeding campaigns for a delegate were usually featured by a fight with Guggenheim against the pioneers as represented by the successful delegate. The latter in one campaign called themselves the "rough-neck" party, adopting a term of reproach used by their opponents.

Bitterness was increased by the Keystone Canyon episode in which concealed gunmen murdered representatives of the Reynolds-Alaska Development Company in Valdez, in their attempt to stop them from opening a right-of-way to the interior. The resulting trial of the murderers was a travesty on justice and the culprits were acquitted.

Meanwhile, the Alaska syndicate, as the J. P. Morgan-Guggenheim Bros. combination was familiarly known, was reaching out its financial tentacles attempting to grasp all the sources of profit in this virgin territory. The purchase of the Alaska Steamship Company in 1902, and the construction of the Copper River and Northwestern Railroad made a transportation monopoly a very real menace to Alaskans. At the same time the fishing industry was almost monopolized by 1904. The largest copper mines were held by the syndicate and efforts were being made to seize all coal lands before the world at large knew that such deposits existed. Capitalism and Guggenheimism were twin red rags that goaded Alaskans into bitter opposition in the early years of this century. Unfortunately, President Roosevelt's policy of conservation, as pushed before the public by his chief forester, Gifford Pinchot, became involved in the fight with capitalism in the minds of Alaskans. Capitalism and conservation were both so abused in Alaska that residents there even now fail to see the many undoubted benefits of both. The whole struggle came to a head in the Ballinger-Pinchot controversy. This dispute arose over the filing of the so-called Cunningham group of coal claims. President Roosevelt had sealed Alaskan coal lands in 1906, on Pinchot's advice, but before this order had gone through Cunningham and a group of associates had filed claims for entry in the Katalla Bay Region. Richard A. Ballinger, former reform mayor of Seattle, as commissioner of the general land office, had the power to pass on the legality of these claims. The investigations of his agent, Glavis, seemed to show that the claimants planned to turn over their coal lands to the Alaskan syndicate. Ballinger adopted a vacillating policy in regard to the claims and dismissed Glavis from service. As Secretary of the Interior, Ballinger continued his policy of opposing conservationists and encouraging the Cunningham claimants. This brought him into direct opposition with Pinchot, who actively took up the cause for Glavis, as both had been dismissed from office. The trial which was started as an attack on the conservationists became, through the brilliancy of Brandeis, later Supreme Court Justice, and Pepper, later Senator, an attack on Secretary Ballinger. The Cunningham claims were finally denied but Ballinger resigned under fire and suffered political death by the controversy. Even President Taft was suspected of connivance in the mess but convincingly cleared himself. The aftermath of the quarrel brought Alaska into national significance, as Roosevelt was powerfully influenced by it to justify his friend Pinchot and the policy of conservation. Consequently, he launched the "Bull Moose" or Progressive Party of 1912 which split the Republican vote and allowed Wilson to win the election.

Meanwhile, in the spring of 1911, the bitterness of Alaskans against conservation in general and Pinchot in particular reached fever heat. Pinchot was burned in effigy and condemned throughout the territory. A party of Cordova citizens, exasperated at being forced for years to pay duty on inferior Canadian coal, while their own deposits lay all around them, marched to the wharf and dumped a cargo of Canadian coal into the bay. This Cordova Coal Party impressed the nation as only such a dramatic act could. But even then many failed to see that it was an expression of the real feeling of the pioneers and not an isolated radical outbreak. The territorial bill of 1913 helped to mollify the Alaskans, and the outbreak of the World War changed the whole aspect of affairs.

An interesting sidelight on the political history of this period was the inane proposal of certain reformers that our Government should cede southeastern Alaska, or the Panhandle, as it was called, to Canada. They urged the act as a token of our good will, and as a means of cleaning our hands so that we might offer ourselves as unselfish arbitrators in the World War. There was much empty talk of the suppressed nationality of the Canadians by our holding the strip of territory barring them from the ocean. The proposal reached the dignity of a House Resolution but was not treated seriously by sane-minded citizens, and remains but another example of the lengths to which theoretical reformers may go in seeking to be their brother's keeper.

Alaskan politics and problems have refused to take a back seat ever since the pre-war legislation. The Taft administration recommended a government railway which was started by the Wilson administration and carried through by Harding. President Harding's visit to the territory in 1923, immediately preceding his death, was the last of a long series of congressional and administration tours of the country that show an increasing desire on the part of our national government to make the rule of Alaska more intelligent and fairer than it has been in the past. The Yukon Territory, Canada's province nearest Alaska, has practically always pointed the way to Alaskans in governmental reform. This sad commentary on United States colonial administration must be corrected before government in Alaska can be said to be intelligent, as the Yukon is inferior in resources and possibilities to Alaska. Much remains to be done governmentally before Alaskans can cease to blame this phase of their life for the present retarded growth.

CHAPTER X

SOCIAL AND INTELLECTUAL GROWTH

SOCIALLY the growth of Alaska has been very rapid and has many peculiarities, due to the fact that it is in the unusual position of being a pioneer country in the twentieth century. The improved means of communication and transportation have made all parts of Alaska easily accessible to the United States, which is one of the most progressive countries of a highly civilized world. Thus, while the outlying parts of the territory present a picture of true pioneer life, with game and fish available in plentiful numbers for the sportsman, and with the rigors that we ordinarily associate with the frontier, at the same time the centers of population are much farther advanced than towns of corresponding size in the United States.

The territory is one of the few big game lands of this modern highly-commercialized world. Despite the foolish slaughter of game by the early residents there is still an abundance of all varieties and under more intelligent protection by locally-made game laws instead of jurisdiction from Washington the game should not be killed off as fast as formerly. The huge Kodiak bear on the Aleutian Peninsula and the island for which it is named annually attracts hunters from all parts of the world. Its quest is considered among the greatest of experiences for world-famed hunters. Practically all other species of bear are found there, including the polar, grizzly, cinnamon and ordinary black bear. Mountain goats, moose, caribou, elk and other varieties of big game are equally prevalent—so much so that the Alaskan railroad has seen fit to stop its trainmen from shooting caribou from their trains while in motion. Moose are as thick on the Kenai Peninsula as domestic cattle on the prairie ranges of the States. Deer remain an important source of food. They have been thinned out noticeably by the wolves and by indiscriminate hunting. Ducks and geese, trout and salmon are there in quantities sufficient to satisfy the most exacting sportsman. The local game law commission combined with the elimination of red tape in bureau control at Washington makes the future of Alaska as a sportsman's paradise an assured one.

Where civilization has reached Alaska, life is of the most advanced type. This is due to the fact that wages are high and money is plentiful, and also to the fact that each town in Alaska is the center of a wide-spread district made up of small industrial settlements dependent upon it. Before the war, wages on the coast ranged from $3.00 to $6.00 per day and living costs were $1.00 to $2.00 a day. In the interior wages of $7.00 to $15.00 per day compared with living costs of $2.00 to $3.00 per day. The scarcity of women and of family life makes the country a poor man's paradise, in that there is little or no destitution and every man can secure work for the asking with no danger of wage cutting by dependent classes. A town of 3,000 inhabitants in Alaska boasts five and six story concrete buildings, three or four theaters, two or three large well-appointed hotels, hundreds of autos and similar marks of a big city, whereas a town of the same population on the Great Plains, or even in New England, would be classed as nothing more than a hamlet. The coast towns can afford every urban refinement, even to golf courses in a town of a population of less than 1,000, as each incorporated town is supported by a score or more of surrounding settlements made up of canneries, mines, logging camps and Indian villages. The interior towns are located for the most part on the sites of old trading posts. These few log huts set up at a convenient fork of the rivers provided a natural center for the cluster of villages springing up in the vicinity. They have retained their pioneer aspect to a greater extent than the coast cities as they are more inaccessible to the refinements of modern civilization. This latter condition is rapidly being changed by the railroads which run the year round on regular schedules; and by the airplane whose use is developing faster in Alaska than almost anywhere else. This peculiar metropolitan character of all Alaskan towns has given the social side of life there an abnormal growth. At the same time education, religion and the other forms of "higher life" are more advanced than in any other pioneer country at a similar stage of development.

As would be expected in a country of great spaces and few people, club life has grown very rapidly. Practically every fraternal organization of the United States is represented there, the Red Men, Masons, Eagles and Elks being especially prominent. Local residents founded the Arctic Brotherhood which for a generation dominated the fraternal field. Captain William A. Connell of the Steamship "City of Seattle" organized a troupe of his passengers while lying in the harbor of Skagway in the winter of 1899. This Arctic Brotherhood was started as a means of passing the time away on trips to and from the United States. At a meeting held in Skagway by travelers held up by ice in the interior the order was made permanent and the first A. B. Hall built there. From these informal beginnings a lodge of thousands of members grew with local chapters in practically every town of Alaska. Theodore Roosevelt, with Captain Connell, were the only life honorary members. The Brotherhood has its home at the Arctic Club, a Seattle skyscraper. The Pioneers of Alaska started an organization in 1908 which includes most of the "sourdoughs" of the territory. This order takes rank with the G. A. R. or other veteran organizations rather than with purely fraternal orders. It centers about the Pioneers' Home maintained at Sitka and numbers in its personnel the makers of Alaskan-United States history.

Religious life far outdistances the club organization. The Russian Orthodox Church had performed yeoman service among the primitive natives under the leadership of Bishop Veniaminoff. Probably the earliest western church in Alaska was the Episcopal, represented by Archdeacon Robert McDonald, who came to the country in 1862. He was followed by such outstanding high churchmen as Archbishop Stuck and Bishop Peter Trimble Rowe. Their mission at Port Hope is one of the northernmost Church stations. The Catholics came to the country in 1877 and throve there due to the direction of Bishop Charles J. Seghers, known as the "Apostle of Alaska." The Holy Cross Mission on the Yukon is their great center in the north. The Presbyterians came into Alaska in greatest numbers and for years dominated the educational field there. Governor Brady came to the country originally as one of their missionaries in 1878 and with his co-workers, Sheldon Jackson and S. Hall Young, exercised almost despotic sway over the natives. The Baptists, Methodists and Moravians also have stories of heroism to relate about their efforts in Alaska. The lone monumental work of Father Duncan with the Tsimpshian Indians of southeastern Alaska has already been mentioned.

Except for the gold stampede era around 1900 the history of civilization in Alaska has chiefly been confined to the coastal regions. Consequently, marine life has bulked large in the story of the country. Gas boats are as necessary to the Alaskan as flivvers to the American. The bulk of the population to-day is dependent for its existence on the wealth that the ocean gives forth and the highways that it provides. Revenue cutter service has been the great handmaiden to the natives of the country. Such famous boats as the "Bear," the "Rush," and the "Gedney" carried on in the uncharted waters for over a half century. They are now being succeeded by such modern palaces as the "Northland." Among their varied duties the crew rate as ordinary tasks rescuing vessels in distress, giving medical aid, enforcing law and order, delivering mail, killing game for starving natives, stopping epidemics and officiating at births, marriages and deaths. One of the colorful phases of marine life left to-day is the

Alaska Packers' sailing fleet which annually sets sail from San Francisco in the spring with raw materials and hundreds of cannery workers. They sail up the North Pacific to their canneries where they tie up at the docks all summer and load the season's pack for the return voyage. These ships, known as the Star Fleet because of their names—"Star of India," "Star of Lapland," et cetera—take three weeks to a month for their voyage each way and number in their list, ships which have sailed for fifty years or more to all ports of the world.

As there were no lighthouses in Alaska before 1900 except the light on Baranof Island at Sitka, and the charting of the waters was never effective until the drag surveys conducted since the war, accidents have been numerous. Starting with the grounding of Vancouver's ship the "Chatham" in 1792, Alaskan history is full of marine disasters. The Hudson Bay boats "Beaver," "Otter" and "Labouchere" all suffered minor accidents but the first major disaster was that of the "Nikolai I" which was a total loss near Kake in 1861. The "Growler," a United States ship, was lost in 1868 with all on board. The steamer "George S. Wright" left Sitka in 1873 and was never heard of again. Too many submerged rocks have been discovered and marked in Alaskan waters at the cost of lives, dollars and ships. One of the most dramatic disasters was that of the "Islander" which in 1901 on a beautifully clear night hit a lone rock with a loss of forty-two lives and a big cargo of gold dust. In more recent years "The State of California" sank with a loss of thirty-five lives, in broad daylight, within a few hundred yards of a cannery. The

"Star of Bengal," one of the sailing fleet, piled up on a reef in 1908 and hundreds lost their lives. In 1898 all manner of old hulks were pressed into service to rush stampeders north, and it is small wonder that thirty of these ships were lost in that year alone. The total fishing craft loss from 1848 to 1914 was $12,792,250 and Alaskan history shows five hundred wrecks in the same period. To-day, there are close to a thousand aids to navigation, such as lighthouses, radio beacons, fog horns, etcetera. This, with the drag survey, which locates the jagged volcanic peaks, has made navigation fairly safe, but the passenger to Alaska, especially in winter, still has many a thrill as the vessel wends its way through tortuous waterways between towering mountains with snow falling thickly about, and the pilot measures his distance from land by timing the echo from his tooting whistle.

While life afloat has proved dramatic as well as useful for residents of the coast towns of Alaska, life ashore has not been without incident. In the rush days a town like Skagway with about 2,000 population could boast 65 saloons. Even down as late as the World War the town of Ketchikan with 2,500 population had 13 saloons. In both cases, the permanent population was no index to the source of income to these institutions but each town was the center of a large floating population exclusively male which led a hardy existence and sought relaxation in whatever form possible. These men with true pioneer roughness did not hesitate to trample on the rights of the natives and all other inferior races. The Orientals have always been particularly despised in the territory. This feeling came to a head in 1886 when miners of Juneau and

Douglas packed the Chinese laborers who had been imported by the Treadwell Mine into two small boats and shipped them south. Governor Swineford tried vainly to have the Orientals return but he was balked on every hand by official and unofficial refusal to take any action. To-day, the Indians are able to hold their own with any other race as they are practically all civilized. Life along the coast is now not so pioneer as it is Scandinavian. The pioneer aspect still remains, however, in the interior. The life is far from being as settled as that of the United States in any section, as indicated by the fact that hardware remained the biggest import as late as 1910. The chief diversions of the coast towns are very similar on a small scale to those of the States. Traveling troupes, moving pictures, the radio, baseball and basket ball, and particularly dances, hold a large part in the social life of those regions accessible to the south. Farther north, dances and moving pictures bulk larger, but even as far north as Fairbanks an annual baseball game played at midnight is a feature of the year.

The great colorful diversion of the north was long the dog race which has lost much of its color because gambling has been prohibited. The first big dog race was held in 1908 with a quarter of a million dollars staked on the outcome. In the days just before the World War the annual dog races ranked as one of the sporting events of the world—real tests of endurance for dog and man, with small fortunes wagered on the favored teams. Allan Alexander Allan or "Scotty" Allan, as he is familiarly known to generations of Alaskans, is the name most prominently connected with this phase of

Alaskan life. Thrice winner of the All-Alaska sweepstakes and noted as the greatest racer and the greatest dog driver that Alaska produced, Allan is a national character. When the World War broke out, although an old man, he enlisted with a team of dogs in the service of France carrying mail in the Alps. His backer, Mrs. E. B. Darling, also looms large in the annals of dog racing and her best lead dog "Baldy" is a real hero in the north. There are numerous other racers who have had their day of fame such as Fox Ramsay, Casson and Leonhard Seppala. The last-named spent twenty-six years in Alaska and was "Scotty" Allan's most apt pupil. He also won the All-Alaska sweepstakes three times—a race 408 miles long from Nome to Candle and return which was the classic of the winter season.

Dog racing reached its dramatic climax in the winter of 1925, when a diphtheria epidemic broke out in the once great mining camp of Nome. The lone doctor of the village feared for the existence of the village itself when his supply of antitoxin was exhausted. His telegraphic appeal for aid started a new supply of serum from Seattle which was rushed by steamer to Seward, thence by rail to Fairbanks, thence by airplane down the Yukon and thence by relay of the best dog teams that the north afforded to Nome. Seppala left Nome intending to rest at Nulato and return with the serum but the relay was so fast that he met the carrier on the outward journey and was forced to turn about to carry the serum over Norton Sound with the thermometer thirty degrees below zero. He carried the serum 120 miles, making his total traveling without rest, 340 miles. Despite the need of

"Scotty" Allan and one of his racing teams.

trusting to the instinct of his dogs on the trackless frozen sea his time was phenomenally fast. His best day was ninety miles and he averaged better than fifty miles a day. The serum reached Nome in time and the incident remains as an epic of the north because the spotlight of world publicity happened to play on it. Needless to say, lives are being saved every year in Alaska in similarly dramatic ways, as the country still remains in many parts a land where men are face to face with the primitive—one of the few real frontiers left in the world.

In recent years there has been a growing tourist trade to the territory, induced in large part by the "See America First" campaign. The creation of Mt. McKinley National Park has attracted to the territory lovers of mountain scenery and mountain climbing. The inland route through southeastern Alaska with its numerous fiords, glaciers and picturesque bays provides an ocean voyage through calm waters that will attract the poorest sailor. Numerous mineral springs add health seekers to the tourist traffic. The combination results in more than 25,000 people visiting Alaska annually. The true value of this trade is hard to estimate. It is certain that Alaska will sell itself, in the sense that each one of these visitors will be a publicity agent for the territory in the future, and inasmuch as Alaska's chief need is settlers such publicity is of the best possible kind. On the other hand, Alaskans are too prone to cater to the immediate benefits from tourist visitors in the summer months, and to neglect comparatively the most lasting and substantial advantages to be secured from catering to capital and industry.

The usual tourist voyages are either a trip to southeastern Alaska, along the famous "Inland Passage" and White Pass, or a trip to southwestern Alaska, which now will perforce include the journey to Fairbanks over the government railroad. As was pointed out earlier, these trips, except for that over the railroad, unfortunately stress the beautiful glaciers of the Alaskan coast line, and tend to give the visitors a false idea of the true character of the territory as a whole. World travelers affirm that the trip to Alaska compares favorably with that to any other part of the world, and it is certain that the tourist traffic will increase rather than diminish in the future.

Intellectually Alaska has developed slowly because such a tremendous virgin area with so scanty a population forced men to be more intent on the physical side of life than on the improvement of their minds. The scarcity of women and the difficulties of communication and transportation in the earlier periods made culture an unknown factor in the nineteenth century history of the country. Even to-day Alaska can boast no native contribution to the world's store of knowledge. On the other hand, the country has been a source of inspiration and a fund of information for numerous scientists and story tellers. Russian occupation, as has already been noted, was chiefly intent on profit—consequently, little of value in a literary or scientific way was produced. Steller, the German naturalist, who accompanied the voyage of discovery, made valuable contributions to scientific literature by his observations. The most ambitious scientific undertaking of the Russians was the Billings expedition which proved more or less of a failure. The early Americans were even more negligent of the finer things of life—so much so that as late as 1887, or twenty years after Alaska became American, the handful of Russians left in the territory were expending more money on their seventeen schools than were the Americans on their whole territorial system, if such a title can be attached to their schools.

Grigor Shelikoff founded the first school in Alaska at Kodiak in 1785. More schools were set up at various other places. The Russian American Company had schools at Sitka and Unalaska and, as has been noted, the total of Russian schools after the purchase was seventeen. The United States government provided for no education whatsoever until after 1884. Church schools were set up for the natives in 1877 chiefly by the Presbyterians and white children attended these as the only opportunity for study. There were no government Indian schools until 1914. Since 1910, education for the whites has progressed rapidly. As soon as towns were allowed to incorporate they secured a means of supporting their schools so that now practically every town and village has a high standard of instruction and a respectable school. To-day, there are over eighty schools with close to five thousand pupils, of whom 669 are high school pupils. Many of the high schools have their graduates admitted to state universities by certificate. This whole system is now headed by the Alaska Agricultural College established at Fairbanks as a means of giving local residents every advantage that the modern world affords.

The period from 1867 to '98 was one of great progress in works on Alaska written, however, almost entirely by non-residents. To this period belong the only histories of Alaska by William H. Dall, the dean of Alaskan scientists, and Bancroft, as part of his series on Pacific Coast history. The voluminous report of Ivan Petroff in 1880 is a classic for information about the territory in that period. Other government reports, such as those by Morris and more particularly by Henry W. Elliott are noted more for their inaccuracies and the opposition they aroused than for any contribution they may afford. The speech of Senator Sumner on the purchase of Alaska remains a classic for the description of the territory at that time. While the days of '98 were days of bitter stress and privation for many, they were at the same time days of romance. Writers and playwrights even to-day who have never been nearer Alaska than a school geography delight in weaving plots around such dramatic times. Among the thousands of stampeders to Alaska there were many who have since preserved their experiences in prose and poetry. Robert W. Service came to the Klondike in his 'teens and while he spent most of his time in Dawson, Canada, his descriptions of the territory are probably the most widely read and the most universally accepted as typical pictures of Alaska. Just as James Fenimore Cooper has painted for us the American Indian as a romantic character who actually never existed but who nevertheless persists in the popular fancy, so Service pictured the unusual in virile poetry that remains the picture that most people carry of Alaska even though it is far from the truth. His "Spell of the Yukon," which has a real basis in fact, "The Shooting of Dan McGrew" and "The Cremation of Sam McGhee" are among the better known of his numerous poems. Jack London wrote eighty-eight works on Alaska including numerous dog stories and he too is guilty of spreading a false gospel of true Alaskan conditions. His "Sea Wolf" is based on a true character, Abe McLean. Rex Beach used historical incidents as the basis for plots of his love stories. "The Spoilers" brings in enough of the sordid life of Judge Noyes to give it a touch of truth but is very far-fetched. "The Iron Trail" opens with a true story of a steamship wreck in southeastern Alaska and centers around the actual fight between the Guggenheims and the Reynolds-Alaska railroad of Valdez for the control of the Keystone Canyon Pass to the interior. Numerous others are listed in the group that have contributed more than 300 works on Alaska. Among the better known are such names as Mark Twain, Washington Irving, Emerson, Hough and Joaquin Miller. It is interesting to note that Jonathan Swift laid his imaginary land of "Brobdingnag" in Alaska when relating the story of Gulliver's Travels. Baron Munchausen, the great liar of fiction, told of visits to the country and probably served as a model to Dr. Cook whose tales of climbing Mt. McKinley and discovering the North Pole made him one of the greatest liars of history.

The advent of the radio, the wireless and the telegraph, together with the steamship and the railroad, have now been completed by the airplane so that all parts of Alaska are in fairly close touch with the outside world at all seasons of the year. Consequently, Alaska's peculiar contributions either intellectually or socially have practically ceased. The country is a small mirror of life in the United States, tempered only by the fact that it is comparatively new to twentieth century conditions.

CHAPTER XI

ECONOMIC DEVELOPMENT

ALASKA'S great problems since 1912 have been economic rather than political, but the economic development of the territory hinges on the policy to be adopted by the political departments at Washington. The problem facing Congress is how to develop the resources in Alaska, and at the same time keep them properly conserved and free from monopolies so as to guarantee Alaska a permanent and stable industrial growth.

In general Alaska had shown a steady, encouraging growth down to and including the World War, but the post-war depression of 1920-21 was accentuated in Alaska for reasons that will be noted and the recovery there has been very slow. The encouraging fact to be noticed is that Alaska will recover and is even now well on the road to her pre-war status. This general economic trend can be shown better probably by noting the outstanding resources of Alaska and their development.

MINING

Furs were the chief source of income to the Russian government while they owned Alaska. They were kept so partially by the fact that Russia was quick to discourage all other forms of industry, especially mining, because she felt that industry would attract settlers and consequently discourage or destroy the fur trade. With the advent of the United States into Alaska all the resources of the country were thrown open to energetic American citizens. As we have noted, prospectors started scouring the hills and vales almost from the time of the purchase. These lone efforts culminated in the rush era. Stampede days gave a tremendous impetus to gold mining in particular and to all mining in a lesser degree. The intensive exploitation of those days and the undue as well as untrue publicity gave the region the glamor of an Eldorado. Such artificial stimulation produced a naturally discouraging aftermath. The easy money stage in Alaskan mining has passed. Time and capital are the great ingredients now necessary to make the future supply slow but steady, keeping pace with demand.

The great extent of mineral resources kept this aftermath from becoming a real decline, and made it rather a period of practically steady returns since 1900 at very nearly the peak production figures of stampede days. For example, the gold output of 1900 was eight million dollars, and that of 1921 was practically the same. The Yukon Valley and Seward Peninsula gold has been largely from placer mining. This is peculiarly the poor man's field. Hence, down to recent years, the output of the region has been produced by many small operators rather than by a few large properties. This condition is now in the period of flux. The rich placers are giving way to lower grade ores, which for their successful development require mining on a large scale, fairly low transportation costs and plenty of capital. The trend seems to be toward dredge mining, and recent discoveries would indicate that dredging can be successfully carried on the year around, even in those sections bordering on the Arctic Circle. At the same time the diminution of rich placers has driven the prospectors to a more intensive search for lode mines—not with the hope of developing their findings themselves, but of disposing of them to capitalists. There are numerous prospects throughout this northern region waiting for capital to be attracted to them, and as soon as mining in the United States reaches a point where large returns on the capital invested are not so certain as they have been, the advent of capital into Alaskan gold mining is likely to follow.

About 1912, the Juneau district, which has been one of the steadiest gold producers of the entire territory, entered upon boom days. The Treadwell Mine, working on low grade ore under large scale production, was still paying large returns. The Alaska Juneau and the Alaska Gastineau Mines were open, and it seemed as though this region was to become a tremendous producer. Failure of the latter property to come up to expectations, and the flooding of the Treadwell Mine in 1917, discouraged capital from entering other parts of Alaska. Juneau is still capable of much more development than is now taking place there, and a slower, healthier growth, which is now in prospect, will regain the confidence of the moneyed interests.

The areas abutting the Alaska Railroad are now being opened up to low grade placer mining because of the increased ease and decreased cost of transportation. It is estimated that there are twenty districts feeding the Alaska

Railroad with placer ore. These employ 1,500 men on an average and the 1924 output was a quarter of a million dollars more than that of 1923. Among such districts are especially the Fairbanks or Tanana fields, the upper, central and lower Yukon and the Kenai Peninsula. The comparative exhaustion of placer mining here will lead to lode mining more rapidly than in other sections because of the easy access to the properties. Many of the gold mines of Alaska are now held by non-residents for speculation rather than immediate development. Such a condition is obviously bad but relief should be looked for in the lapse of time rather than in an attempt at artificial stimulation by legislation.

Copper is one of the great minerals of Alaska. Its total production of over $135,000,000 under American control down to 1921 ranks on a par with that of gold placer and gold lode mining. The decline in the market value of copper since 1917 has made the annual production appear less than it really is, as it is usually computed in terms of the monetary return. But production if anything is greater than in any other period in the history of the country. Despite low prices the production for 1921 was well over $7,000,000. The focal point of the copper production of Alaska is the Kennecott Mine at Cordova in southwestern Alaska. This great property of the Guggenheims is one of the ranking copper mines of the world. Some idea of its richness can be gained from the fact that it had one vein 100′ long and 80′ wide which produced about 70% pure copper. At the present time it has forty miles of underground workings with a pay roll of $90,000 a month and its production is three-fourths to nine-tenths of the total Alaska copper output.

Alaskans are inclined to attribute much of their trouble in copper to the fact that the Alaska Steamship Company—a Guggenheim corporation—provides one of the chief means of transportation from the territory, and also controls the only convenient smelter at Tacoma, Washington. Just previous to the war there was only one copper mine operating in Alaska outside of this combine. Prices were so fixed, this operator claimed, that even though producing a rich ore he was unable to operate at a profit. Such charges must be taken in moderation, as it is evident that, once Alaskan copper and gold have gained the place in the world that they deserve, competition will enter the field regardless of how strong the monopoly holdings may appear to be.

Coal has been a known deposit in Alaska from the earliest times. The first mine was worked on Cook Inlet in 1854 by the Russians. Whalers on their way to the Arctic Ocean were in the habit of stopping at coal veins which showed on the coast line in order to secure enough fuel for their voyages into the Arctic. The Cape Lisburne and Point Barrow fields were especially used in this way from 1881 down to modern times. Nevertheless, all of this development was of a very petty and haphazard nature. The great factor influencing the history of Alaskan coal mining has been the policy of conservation. In 1906, coal entries were forbidden for a period of ten years and coal discoveries have always been restricted in one way or another so that natural development has been practically impossible. The known coal deposits of Alaska are equal in quantity to those of Pennsylvania. While they range from lignite to anthracite they are generally of inferior quality to that of the eastern states. It is believed that the Arctic slope when fully explored geologically will yield a much greater quantity than that already known. The Alaska Railroad has operated solely on coal taken from mines along the right of way. These mines—notably the Matanuska and Nenana—produced chiefly a poor grade of bituminous, but anthracite has been found, as well as a higher grade of bituminous. The northern fields are very extensive. The chief problem concerning them is the solution of a means to carry power long distances in Arctic regions.

The average production of coal from 1917 to 1925 was 79,000 tons a year, making a total of close to 800,000 tons for the period. In 1925 over 90,000 tons were produced by the fields bordering the Alaska Railroad alone. Meanwhile Alaska was importing over two million tons, showing that much of Alaska's future coal development can be used to supply local industrial needs. The sole discordant note in this picture of the future of Alaska's coal was sounded by Gifford Pinchot who made a short trip of inspection to Alaska for President Taft in the fall of 1911. The burden of his report was, "Alaska coal is less likely to dominate the Pacific Coast market than had been thought when the fields were first discovered." Yet at the same time Pinchot was straining every nerve even to the extent of getting his political friends to conserve this Alaskan resource. His action does not seem to be logical unless we consider that he was seeking to check the cupidity of capitalists aiming to exploit this new region. Since 1916 the government leasing system seems more intelligently designed to aid development of the coal industry.

Silver, tin, quicksilver, marble, lead, cinnabar, platinum, cement and numerous other minerals have been discovered and are being developed commercially in all parts of the territory. This all shows that Alaska will not be dependent for her mineral growth on any one resource but that her mining will be diversified enough to guarantee a healthy, permanent industry. From 1880 to 1927 Alaskan mines produced roughly $590,000,000. Less than half of this was placer gold which would include the gold rush output. The industry has gone through successive stages—first from 1880 to '98 the period of low grade, lode gold mining particularly at Treadwell; from '98 to 1906 the placer mining rushes of the upper Yukon after the Klondike and at Nome; from 1906 to 1915 the central Yukon placer mining centering in the Fairbanks fields which produced $22,000,000 in 1906 alone; from 1915 to 1927 the copper mining period led by Kennecott, which in 1916 produced about $30,000,000; from 1927 the gold dredging period made possible by the Alaska railway and the discovery of a cold water thawing process. The last period is one requiring capital and leading to diversification of output. Conservative geologists such as A. H. Brooks say that it is not too much to predict that the future growth of Alaska's minerals will be as great as the past, if not greater. They estimate that there is $17,000,000,000 in minerals still in Alaska.

The history of oil is very much like that of coal. The oil lands were closed from 1910 to 1920, and since then have been opened on a leasing system, which has been proved to be faulty in some respects but is certainly better than complete conservation. This governmental discouragement was intensified by the adverse effect of the Panama Canal and the boom in California oil. The Bering River oil fields, near Katalla, are the only fields developed extensively to date. The oil produced there from eleven operating wells averaged about forty barrels per day in 1922. It is a paraffin base oil of as good quality as that of Pennsylvania and twice as good as the average oil of the United States. The development of most of the other oil fields of Alaska has been hampered by lack of properly surveyed lands, and hence the inability of prospective drillers to secure a clear title to their holdings. The Arctic slope certainly has extensive oil prospects, but it appears now as though the Cold Bay Region, and the Alaskan Peninsula in general, would be the probable center of the future oil industry of Alaska.

Fishing

The history of Alaskan fishing from 1890 down to 1922 is a story of senseless exploitation by private interests running rampant. It has been said that Americans are the worst offenders of all nationalities in their failure to realize that no natural resources can be developed to the utmost and still continue to provide a good revenue. Certainly the fishing operators of Alaska bear out this contention to the fullest. The fisheries of Alaska were probably originally among the richest of any section of the world. Salmon, halibut, whales, cod, herring and numerous other species literally packed the coastal waters and numerous streams of southeastern and southwestern Alaska. Throughout Russian occupation these fisheries, except the whale, were used almost exclusively for local consumption. Salting, smoking or drying were the sole means of preserving the fish.

The first cannery came in 1878 at Klawack in southeastern Alaska. This was followed by the advent of numerous private operators so that in 1890 there were 37 canneries and salteries, and almost an equal number of owners. By 1892, consolidation had reduced the number of competitors to a half dozen, while the total number of plants continued to increase. This consolidation was not wholly an evil, inasmuch as individual competition had given rise to many disturbances. Barricades, wire screens and dams in the streams were common evils of the day. The poor labor conditions led to Indian outbreaks, and all this was made worse by the fact that the Government had few responsible parties to enforce their decrees upon. The Alaska Packers' Association was one of the earliest and largest fish trusts of Alaska. Some idea of the extent of their control may be gained from the fact that they packed at least half the total output of Alaska, and their opening quotations established the market prices. Their control was so all-inclusive that the governor's reports and the reports of special agents were based upon their records. The Alaska Pacific Fisheries, the Pacific Packing and Navigation Company and the Booth Fisheries were other large corporations to enter the field at about this time.

In the early days of the industry the labor supply had been chiefly from the local residents or Americans from the Pacific Northwest, but the large scale operators introduced Chinese in great numbers after 1906. These Chinese were secured in the Pacific Coast cities under a contract system. The corporation guaranteed to pay the Chinese agent a certain price per case for a fixed number of cases. If the pack fell short of the guarantee the company had to make up the deficit; if it surpassed it the Chinese were paid at the same rate for all extra cases packed. This system of absentee production took hold of Alaska. These operators would send their crews and supplies north in the late spring, fish Alaskan waters intensively throughout the summer, at the same time packing cases of salmon into the large sailing vessels tied at the cannery wharves. Then in the early fall they would bundle their whole season's work and workers into their ships and sail away for the States, leaving Alaska nothing except a nominal sum for taxes on the deserted cannery buildings. For example, between 1893 and 1908, while the canneries were making ten million dollars they paid in all only one-half million dollars in taxes.

The center of Alaska salmon fishing down to 1900 was around Kodiak and Chignik in southwestern Alaska. As this region became depleted around 1898 operators moved more and more toward southeastern Alaska. Along with this gradual taking up of all the eligible locations for cannery sites went an increase in the devices for catching salmon. Standing traps stretching out into the sea one hundred yards or more were so designed as to catch the salmon as soon as they entered the inland waterways and long before they reached their spawning grounds in the streams. Floating traps, which were more economically built, were introduced to accomplish the same result in more accessible places.

The World War increased the demand for salmon and brought to a crisis the exploitation of commercial salmon fishing in Alaska. By 1920 Alaska was the source of more than half the world's annual supply of canned salmon. The industry had already produced well over a half billion dollars since the purchase of Alaska and in 1920 alone produced over forty million dollars. There were about 25,000 people engaged in the industry, and in the peak year of 1918, 101,000,000,000 salmon were caught.

Some feeble attempts at conservation started in 1889 and had gone on throughout the early years of the century. By an act of 1906, the canners were given a rebate of four cents per case on their packs for every thousand fry liberated by private hatcheries. Under this provision many hatcheries were installed by the larger corporations and some few by individual operators, but the operators themselves admitted that old style hatcheries were impractical for red salmon and only partially successful for king salmon and humpback. Hatchery salmon when released were unable to protect themselves as well as the fish which spawned naturally as they had not learned the valuable law of self-preservation—consequently, their subsequent loss of life was much greater than that of non-hatchery fish.[1] The habits and characteristics of the fish are now carefully studied and they are reared as naturally

[1] A. J. Sprague, Superintendent of Alaska Hatcheries.

7
8
6
3
4
2
1
5
2

SALMON TRAPS

These traps are built on the knowledge that salmon follow a given course in the water and very seldom turn in their own wake. Their course is usually along the shore line until they strike an obstruction such as the "lead" of a trap. They then follow the lines of the trap. These traps are usually built out into the water about 100 feet, and two or three of them along the shore in the approach to a salmon stream very soon catch all of the salmon frequenting that stream—hence, unrestricted, they are a great menace to the fish. The principle of the floating trap is the same as the standing here depicted except that pipes hung from the logs displace the piles. The floating trap is more mobile but less efficient.

1. The lead, which is a straight line of stakes or piles running at right angles to the shore line from which wire or net webbing is hung, from higher than the tide mark to the ocean bottom.

2. Hearts. These are V-shaped and turned slightly toward the lead, starting thirty to forty feet on either side and running in the same general direction. Usually traps have a big or outer heart with a supplementary inner heart, the narrow end of the latter leading to the pot. Some traps have only one.

3. Tunnel. A long opening, narrow up and down, held in position by ropes and rods. Below this:

4. The apron—a sheet of web netting stretched from the bottom of the heart upward to the pot, to lead into the pot fish which are swimming low in the water and to obviate building the pot to the ocean bottom. Some traps have:

5. Jiggers, on each side or one side of the heart, which help turn the fish into the channel.

6. The pot. A square compartment behind the inner heart with web walls and bottom connected in the shape of a large square sack, hauled up and down by ropes and tackles at the four corners.

7. Spiller. Another square compartment adjoining either end of the pot, or both, and simply the fish container.

8. A small tunnel which leads the fish from the pot to the spiller, whence the fishermen lift them on to the scows for transportation to the cannery. This last operation is known as brailing, and consists simply of raising the web bottom to sufficient height to dump the fish directly into the pots.

and freely as possible. They all agree that a closed season combined with intelligent hatchery work is the best preservative.

The visit of President Harding and part of his cabinet to Alaska resulted in the Act of 1922 setting up fishing reservations under the Department of Commerce. Under this act the salmon pack was limited in certain localities. The Alaskan Delegate, Dan Sutherland, strenuously objected to these regulations, contending that the limit was too high and that large corporations were given exclusive rights. He even went to the extent of labeling the new regulations as a grab and laid the blame for the grab on Dr. Charles Henry Gilbert, Professor of Zoology at Leland Stanford University. He then enlarged on this point by reminding Congress that F. B. Anderson, Chairman of the Finance Committee of Stanford, was a Director of the Alaska Packers' Association and that Herbert Hoover, a Regent of Stanford, sanctioned the regulations as Secretary of Commerce.[1] He presented such strong statements as this: "Russian sealing records of 1800-1834 have been deliberately falsified by the report of Dr. David Starr Jordan on fur seal investigations, parts 1-4, 1898. Jordan and his associates did this to conceal the truth as to the ruinous work of land killing by the lessees on the Pribilof Islands." [2] Sutherland recommended the passage of laws similar to those in vogue in other countries but his objections and ideas were dismissed as the rant of a politician. Probably

[1] Speech of Delegate Sutherland, House of Representatives, Feb. 28, 1923. Cong. Record, Vol. 64, p. 4942.

[2] House Comm. on Expenditures in the Dept. of Commerce, April 14, 1914.

his fears were justifiable in that the reservations were not set up after mature enough study. At the same time, such extravagant censure as he allowed himself to indulge in was not defensible. By a further Act of 1924, the Secretary of Commerce was given full authority to limit or prohibit any or all fishing operations and to set up rules and regulations for fishing. Secretary Hoover, acting under this authority, set up stringent regulations entirely prohibiting fishing in seventy-six localities in Alaska, and closely restricting fishing in all other districts. The exact value of these regulations is hard to ascertain in so short a time of trial. The tendency of Alaskans was to extol Hoover as the savior of Alaska's fisheries. The season of 1926 with a pack of 6,652,882 cases seemed to add the seal of prosperity to Hoover's work and Alaskans were ready to erect monuments to such a guardian of their resources. 1927, however, showed a decrease of almost 50% in the annual pack, and the fishery authorities were at a loss to explain such a falling off. The sum and substance of the experiment seems to be that while legislation was entirely desirable we are unable to judge whether that already decided upon is wise or not until after several years have elapsed—at least, the four years which make up the ordinary cycle of salmon life.

The canning industry under the attention of Washington authorities should become stabilized probably at the point it has now reached of around 130 canneries with over $60,000,000 invested and employing between 20,000 and 25,000 employees. The expansion of the fishing industry in the future will probably come in frozen fresh fish rather than canning.

This process is especially adapted to conditions in southwestern Alaska and the Aleutian Islands, hence its growth will renew the producing value of an area once exhausted. Even under unrestricted private operations Alaska's salmon fisheries were not in danger of absolute extermination but were certainly threatened with extermination as a commercial field. The development now seems to be toward large corporations and mergers even extending to mergers of eastern and western fisheries so as to guarantee a steady diversified market output throughout the year.

The whaling industry which in 1857 boasted 300 ships, fell off by 1881 to 30 ships. This was due, first of all, to the fact that the industry was not protected by the government, and secondly, to the decreased demand for oil because of the discovery of oil wells. To-day there are only three whaling stations in Alaska. The whalers of old were a romantic crew chasing the great Bowhead in small, frail ships. These whales would produce around 275 barrels of oil and 3,500 pounds of bone. The advent of the Standard Oil Company has changed the pursuit to that of the Humpback and the Sulphur Bottom, whose products are an oil used in cosmetics, fertilizer and an occasional find of ambergris.

In 1867, twenty-three vessels made a catch of cod worth $350,000. This product has remained about the same, the cod catch of 1919 being valued at about a half million dollars.

Halibut fishing grew slowly to 1895 when it first took on commercial importance. Since then it expanded rapidly until in 1925 over ten million pounds of halibut were caught in the Gulf of Alaska and adjacent waters. The largest halibut fleet in the world, numbering 300 vessels, now fishes the Gulf of Alaska. The danger of extermination here was averted by the North Pacific Halibut Treaty of March, 1923, by which the United States and Great Britain agreed to an annual closed season from November 16 to February 16. The latest menace to this industry is increasing Japanese competition which Alaskans wish to curb.

The herring industry is comparatively recent in Alaska, but already employs a thousand workers and the annual pack runs well into the millions of dollars. The quality of Alaskan herring is equal to that of Norwegian, and this fishery will one day rival that of the salmon and halibut. A picturesque feature of the herring industry is the fact that the bulk of the employees are Scotch lassies imported for their skill in packing these smaller fishes by hand.

Shrimp, clam and crab factories are operating in different parts of Alaska, making the fisheries of the territory rank on a par with mining, both in total value of production and diversity of product.

Furs

While the fur resources of Alaska are nowhere near the value of Russian days, they are still a substantial factor in the economic life of the territory, and there is no reason to believe that they will ever be exterminated, particularly in the more inaccessible parts of the territory, and in those sections where mining or oil drilling is the chief industry. After the seal monopoly of the Alaska Commercial Company was closed in 1890, it was found that the seal herd was badly depleted. In spite of the settlement of the Bering Sea dispute this depletion continued, so that the government in 1910 took over complete control of the Pribilof Islands as the sole effectual way of properly protecting this valuable resource.

The Department of Commerce employs the natives of the Pribilof Islands to kill only 95% of the three-year-old males annually, leaving the rest of the herd for natural increase. The seal herd was further protected by the treaty of December 15, 1911, by which Great Britain, Japan, Russia and the United States agreed to stop all pelagic sealing except that of natives for their own food, and even these are not allowed to kill with firearms. No one is allowed to land on the islands at any time. Under the treaty the United States must give Japan and Canada each 15% of the season's catch. Russia also guarantees to give the same countries 15% of her kill on the Commander Islands and the Japanese agree to give 10% to the United States, Russia and Canada of any kill on their islands. Great Britain also contracts to give the same percentage, but the likelihood of any seals landing on the islands owned by England is so small that we can practically say that the United States and Russia have paid for the protection of their rookeries. This prohibition of pelagic sealing extends over the Pacific Ocean and Bering Sea north of 30 degrees. The treaty was signed for a period of fifteen years and for successive periods until ended by a twelve months' notice given by one or more of the contracting parties. The Japanese government has asked for a conference on this treaty but none has yet been held and it continues in force.

Under governmental control the herd is rapidly increasing. In 1912 it numbered 215,000 and in 1925, 723,050. The islands now produce a million dollar crop of seals a year and about two million dollars is being added to the value of the island farm annually. The annual catch is auctioned each spring at St. Louis. At the World Fur market in 1923, in three hours over 18,000 skins were sold for close to $600,000. The 1924 sale of 25,395 brought over $700,000. Thus the long-vexed question of the Alaska fur seal seems to have been definitely settled and a permanent industry guaranteed.

Of the other Alaskan furs, the fox is rapidly taking front rank, particularly the blue fox, due chiefly to the great increase in fox farming. Fox farms were started as early as 1886 by the Alaska Commercial Company on the islands near the Pribilofs and by 1901 thirty islands had been stocked. This industry seems to offer an attractive field for investment. The necessary items include a small island which can be leased from the government for a nominal sum and can be handled by a keeper with one or two assistants. The islands are secured for a three-year exploration period at the end of which the forest service makes an appraisal and fixes the annual rental charge. The term is then renewable for a period of fifteen years. When the industry was beginning, little was known regarding the kinds of food necessary or the soil and rock formations suitable for denning. But with all of these difficulties the profits were enormous and the industry so attractive that by 1926 there were close to four hundred farms in Alaska containing over 36,000 foxes with a total capital investment of $6,000,000. In 1925, the fox sale at St. Louis of 1,800 skins was over $50,000. Successful fox farms have led Alaskans into all manner of fur farming. The most practical seems to be mink farming as these animals are easily raised and the chance of loss is small. Artificial fur cultivation should be easily stabilized and guarantee Alaska an industry in the field regardless of how populous the country may become. The first great Alaskan fur was the sea otter. From 1743 to 1799 the Russians had secured 186,754 otters and 100 ships were engaged in this business. To-day the animal is almost extinct because of such tremendous free fishing. By the seal treaty of 1911, the sea otter was also protected so that its future increase can be expected. The marten, sable, lynx, weasel, bear, beaver and muskrat are other furs produced in Alaska in commercial quantities. The total annual fur sale of Alaska is well over three million dollars at the present time, and here again the industry may be regarded as a stable one with an assured permanent future.

Pulp and Timber

In general the timber of Alaska has a prospective value chiefly for pulp and paper. The lumbering possibilities are necessarily limited due to high transportation costs because of distance, and the inferior quality of the timber. The first steam saw mill in Alaska was at Sitka in 1878, operated by the boiler from the naval ship "Jamestown." Before that, Russians had whipsawed or hewn logs for their vessels.

Hand logging was very extensive in the early days and continued even down to 1900; steam logging to-day has not penetrated far into the forests but is mostly carried on within 2,000 feet of shore. The only true forest section is that of southeastern Alaska. The Yukon Valley is studded with islands of forests but not in commercial quantities. The forests are fairly free from the natural dangers of fires or insects but are over mature and should be cut at once, especially the spruce, so as to allow young trees to grow. The line of virgin timber in the world recedes more rapidly than any other line before civilization and the zone of economic production of lumber has already reached Alaska. Alaskan mills are now shipping lumber to the Orient, Australia and Hawaii, but the bulk of their product is still locally consumed in fish boxes, barrels and building materials. Two paper mills will be in operation there by 1932. Ninety-five per cent of the forests are hemlock and spruce, both excellent paper-making woods. These are accessible to tide water and protected channels—hence available for cheap water transportation and cheap water power, and the climate guarantees year-around logging manufacture and shipment. With the federal government in close supervision the use will be so regulated as to guarantee a permanent industry. The two mills now going in will require an investment of between eight and ten million dollars which is large for a new country, but the investment is protected by a guarantee of enough timber to supply a five hundred ton paper mill running throughout the year for fifty years.

There are almost twenty million acres of forests containing

eighty billion feet of timber in southeastern Alaska alone, and the Forestry Service estimates conservatively that the Tongass forest is capable of a permanent industry producing one-third the present pulp consumption of the United States. The possibilities of a future pulp industry have already been demonstrated by many successful mills in the neighboring territory of British Columbia. The fact that there is at least 400,000 horse power in units up to 32,000 h. p. available in southeastern Alaska and that minerals such as pyrite and limestone needed in the industry are convenient, adds to the certainty that there will be a considerable pulp and paper industry in this region before many years.

Reindeer

Dr. Sheldon Jackson of the Presbyterian Church imported sixteen reindeer from Lapland in 1891 as an experiment, seeking to aid the starving Esquimaux who had been deprived of their means of subsistence by the coming of civilization. From that time until 1900, the government imported 1,280 of these animals with a few Laplanders as keepers. This herd, starting at Teller on Seward Peninsula and spreading into the interior, has increased until there are now 350,000 animals distributed in over a hundred Alaskan herds grazing over 2,000 miles, from Point Barrow to the Kuskokwim River. For the most part these are controlled by the Government and let out to Esquimaux herders. The Lomen Company has built up a private herd of over 100,000 head, and in 1926 shipped 5,000 to Seattle and Minneapolis. The government station, founded in 1920, has aided in studying the habits and care of the reindeer. They estimate that Alaska has the territory and food to support three or four million reindeer. The meat is very much like mutton, and without doubt will prove an important source of food supply to Alaska and possibly to the United States in the future. Reindeer meat has been introduced into the American markets but the price is still too high to make it anything but a luxury. As the supply increases and the price is lowered from the present one of about a dollar a pound, the meat will certainly have a favorable reception in the diet of Americans.

Agriculture

Alaskans clearly recognize that their territory can never support a permanent population of any magnitude unless it is able to produce at least the major portion of the food supply at home. The government attacked this problem early by establishing experimental stations in southeastern and southwestern Alaska and the Yukon Valley. The available agricultural land is estimated at about 50,000 square miles for farming and 50,000 square miles in addition for grazing. Southeastern Alaska is best adapted to berries and vegetables but too wet for grains. Southwestern Alaska and the Aleutian Islands are admirably suited for grazing; while grains are raised most easily in the interior, particularly in the Tanana valley. The experimental stations have demonstrated that most of the common agricultural products can be raised successfully in Alaska. They have introduced Siberian wheat and other products calculated to adapt themselves

Herd of Reindeer in northern Alaska.

most readily to Alaskan conditions. The Tanana valley now raises enough potatoes and wheat to take care of all local needs. The farm at Holy Cross, four miles from the Arctic Circle, is one of twenty acres and supports the orphanage of 165 children there.

It is certain, however, that the agricultural resources of Alaska are not sufficient to attract farmers with the idea of developing an export trade. The question as to whether Alaska can support her own population is probably best answered by a comparison with Scandinavian countries. Alaska and Scandinavia have so much in common that the present conditions in the latter may justly be regarded as a forecast of Alaska at a similar age of development. The climates are about the same, especially in the vicinity of the big centers of population. Stockholm and Christiania enjoy the same year-around conditions of Seward and Cordova or Valdez. To-day Sweden has a population of over five million, fifty-five per cent agricultural, and exports $12,000,000 worth of agricultural products annually. Norway and Finland together show a proportionate figure. Alaska's total area is equal to all three countries and her potential agricultural area is greater. Under the circumstances, there is no reason why the future of Alaska agriculturally can be doubted. From 1900 to 1910 the total number of farms in Alaska increased from a dozen to over two hundred with 4,450 acres. It is probable that the chief crops will be potatoes and hardy grains, though cauliflower, cabbage and numerous other crops have been raised successfully. The soil has a limited plant food, hence the chief problem will be to renew the soil either by letting it lie fallow or by increasing the fertilizer. To date the experiments can be characterized as encouraging rather than highly successful, but it would appear evident that Alaska's growth will not be hampered by agriculture inasmuch as the territory will produce food enough to support any population that may be attracted there.

The agricultural development of Alaska will be gradual and will come only with the increase in population stimulated artificially like that of Canadian agriculture and will be dependent for its local market on the growth of industry, the extension of railroads and the building of new highways. It cannot be regarded as an added resource of Alaska in world trade but at the same time it cannot be regarded as a drawback to Alaska's future.

CHAPTER XII

MODERN ALASKA

The perennial song of Alaskans has always been one of optimism and rosy predictions as to the future of the country when the resources were developed as they should be. Such hopes seemed justified as long as Alaska's growth was steady and fairly rapid. The 1910 census of Alaska showed the largest population in her history—64,356. This figure was arrived at after a very accurate survey and may justly be regarded as a minimum. The 1920 census recorded only 55,036 and was equally accurate as a minimum figure. Both counts were taken in midwinter when the permanent population alone remained in the country. This drop of almost 10,000 in population was very disconcerting to Alaskans and those interested in the future of the territory. The wiseacres, who had decried the possibilities of the territory from the time of the purchase onward, seized upon the decrease as an indication that Alaska and her resources were exhausted. They interpreted the figures as showing the limits of Alaskan development and urged the neglect of the country by our government. The decrease of population was discouraging even though two Canadian provinces in the same period had lost four to five times as many people. Americans had been used to greeting each census with enthusiasm over the tremendous increases noted in all parts of the United States and any deviation from this picture was a shock. An analysis of the figures and the reasons for the decrease show that the territory, while temporarily on the down grade, is not beginning a permanent loss of population but is even now gradually recovering from this seeming setback.

The World War may justly be regarded as a chief factor in Alaska's retrogression. During and after the war many people left because of army enlistment, the attraction of higher wages in the States, and the detraction of less prosperity in Alaska because of the sharp drop in demand for two of her greatest products—copper and salmon. These two products equal more than half of Alaska's exports. The salmon export which had been $50,000,000 in 1918 was barely half that figure in 1921, and the copper export showed an even more alarming decrease. The abnormal conditions induced by the war created losses in all parts of the country. That Alaska failed to recover as rapidly as other sections has been explained by Alaskans on the ground that poor transportation facilities and bureaucratic government control have hampered natural recovery. These reasons all have weight and they may be further strengthened by the possibility that many Alaskans, who had been hanging on hoping for better things after the boom days, had received this war depression as the final blow and had definitely decided to leave the territory. This last supposition is more plausible if we remember that the bulk of the loss of population was in single white men and foreign born. The native born are increasing as well as the number of females, both of which are stable elements of population. While the mining towns notably decreased in this period the shipping towns increased.

The number of homesteads increased in ten years to three times the average of 1915. Imports and exports as a whole increased normally despite the decided drop already noted in copper and salmon. Furs showed an especially great increase. By and large it would appear as though Alaska were getting rid of the final vestige of boom days and settling down to a slow, steady, permanent growth. Alaska's greatest needs to-day to insure this growth are immigrants, a reformed transportation system, a simplification of government, and capital.

Improved transportation will attract more people to the territory and will hold more people there through the winter months, as the closer contact with the outside world will make living conditions there more attractive. Payments for a large share of Alaskan exports are never received in Alaska because of the prevalence of absentee capitalism. This condition must be rectified to insure a more prosperous Alaska. The problem of transportation has faced the territory ever since it began to assume commercial importance in North America at the beginning of the century. Congressmen interested in the territory begged for transportation to open up resources, from the time of the purchase onward. Freight and passenger rates were attacked as excessive as early as 1903 and roads were urged in the Senate in that year. Presidents Roosevelt and Taft both saw this need and advocated a government railroad as early as 1906. Both Republican and Democratic governors annually urged more and better transportation in their reports. A. H. Brooks, an authority on Alaskan minerals, sums up his concept of Alaska's mineral wealth by saying that regardless of how tremendous it may be it has no value except as it is made accessible by railways and roads.

Private enterprise had built about three hundred miles of railroad prior to the war. One of the earliest projects for a railroad was that of Harry de Windt for a railroad from the United States to Europe by way of a tunnel at Bering Strait. This project never went beyond the visionary stage. Local mine railways sprang up in all parts of the territory, but private initiative was hampered by a prohibitive tax of one hundred dollars per mile of operation. It is doubtful whether any other pioneer railroad ever had a similar handicap to face in the history of the world. The largest early roads were the White Pass and Yukon from Skagway, at the head of ocean transportation in southeastern Alaska, to White Horse, the head waters of the Yukon River; the Copper River Railroad from Cordova to the Kennecott Copper Mine; and the Alaska Northern from Seward across the Kenai Peninsula. Government action up to the time of the war had been confined to road building, which was not hard surfaced and hence of no use for heavy traffic in the open season. The railroads able to run throughout the year could handle the heavy materials in winter, when they could be transported over the frozen roads and thereby make year-round industry practical throughout Alaska. A road 370 miles long from Valdez to Fairbanks was opened in 1900 and marks the high point of government road building which, by 1927, totalled over 7,000 miles of roads and trails. The latest addition to transportation in Alaska has been the airplane which has been developed commercially as much in that country as anywhere in the United States. There are over forty landing fields in Alaska to-day and a score or more of airplanes make hundreds of trips, carrying passengers and express over thousands of miles. Conditions in Alaska are ideal for flying in almost any season of the year because of the unusual visibility.

The greatest boon to Alaskan transportation was the government railroad. The interest of President Taft led to the authorization by Woodrow Wilson of the first railroad commission in 1912. The government railroad resulting from the investigations of this and subsequent commissions was built from Seward, an open port on the Gulf of Alaska, to Fairbanks in the Yukon Valley. This road started operations in 1923 and should prove the heart of the future transportation system of Alaska. It has cost the United States $62,000,000 so far and it is estimated that $11,000,000 more is necessary for the completion of the road, the total being more than double the original estimate. Add to this the fact that the railroad is suffering an annual deficit, which in 1924 was one and three-quarters millions and in 1925 one and one-quarter million dollars, and you have a sorry picture. The managers cannot definitely say when the road will go on a paying basis, as such a date is dependent on the growth of the territory and the permanent completion of the railroad. John E. Ballaine, a pioneer railroad builder of Alaska, has attacked the government handling of this railroad and blames them for much of the loss already noted. He maintains that the railroad is a failure to date because, first, the Anchorage terminals are far too elaborate and were a useless outlay in the beginning, as no good harbor is available at that point; secondly, he charges the government with failure to develop the country tributary to the road; and finally, he attacks the freight rates which are two to eight times as high as in the United States. His criticism points out the waste of over a half-million dollars in laying out a town for mining coal for the use of the Navy before proper explorations were made as to the accessibility of the coal to the site of the town. In common with other Alaskans he brings into his attack a condemnation of other capitalists, who have continually hampered or blocked the efforts of the government to solve Alaska's transportation problems. He maintains that the waste of the Alaska railroad will total close to forty million dollars by the time it is completed. In the course of his criticisms he attacks many of Alaska's prominent executives as tools of the moneyed interests, including in his diatribe Governors Clark, Hoggatt, Riggs and Bone, and involves Secretaries of the Interior Lane and Fall in his accusations. He compares the rates from Seattle to Alaska as being two and one-half to three times those from Seattle to New York, which is six times as far away, and four times the rate from Seattle to China, which is five times as far.

There is no question but what public funds were wasted in the construction of the Alaskan Railroad. Such mistakes cannot be rectified now, but the government should make every effort to make the road a paying enterprise by adjusting freight rates to attract settlers and industry. The main line of the government railroad is 543 miles long, about the same as the distance from Chicago to Pittsburgh on the Pennsylvania Railroad main line. The highest point on the road is lower than the summit of the trans-continental railroads. Two trains are operated weekly both ways from Seward to Fairbanks carrying full equipment throughout the year, and the road suffers surprisingly few mishaps. The cost of the road at first sight appears enormous but it is low compared with the huge land grants made to our early western railroads, and also it is low if we take into account that Alaska is the greatest per capita contributor to the national resources and has turned in a direct profit to the United States government of close to twenty million dollars. The purchase and maintenance cost of the Philippine Islands to the United States from 1898 to 1910 was $500,000,000; the purchase and maintenance cost of Alaska from 1867 to 1910 was $15,500,000; the receipts from Alaska in the same period were $460,000,000. Hence the railroad, whatever its cost, is a small return for the benefits that Alaska has bestowed upon the parent country and, connecting as it does the interior of Alaska with the ocean, the road should increase these benefits many fold.

This government railroad has only partially solved Alaska's transportation problem. There still exists the evil, either real or imagined, of monopoly control of steamship transportation from the United States. Steamship transportation is a major problem when we remember that there are over 5,000 miles of inland navigable waters in Alaska, and that Seattle is thousands of miles from Alaskan ports, over which the sole means of transportation is by water. In considering Alaska's transportation problem we should remember that the ordinary sailing time from Seattle to the nearest port of Ketchikan is three days, from Seattle to Seward, the railroad terminus, is eight days, and from Seattle to Nome, nine days. Moreover, the customary voyage from Ketchikan to Nome is longer than from Seattle to Nome, and from Seward to points on the Aleutian Islands as long as from Seward to the United States.

As with every other problem of Alaskan history the pioneers attacked the lobbies of these steamship companies maintained at Washington and pointed out the lack of adequate service and the discriminatory rates maintained by the companies. Two companies now hold a monopoly over Alaskan transportation, though there is no evidence of interlocking directorates. Their rates, particularly for freight, are much higher than those between other Pacific ports. The companies plead lack of steady business and seasonal peaks as their excuse. Transportation rates, both by land and by sea, at the present time are not, to say the least, conducive to growth in Alaska. The solution often suggested is a government steamship line. This is very unlikely in view of the great deficit being suffered by the railroad.

The second factor hampering the growth of Alaska is the question of governmental control from Washington, D. C. Throughout the history of the country too much government in the sense of too many bosses in Washington has been a crying evil. Every problem that arose in Alaska seemed to give official Washington an excuse to add another bureau to the control of the territory, until every branch of the executive department has a finger in the government and, what is far worse, each cabinet officer controls his portion of Alaska through several different bureaus. An extreme example is the fact that the brown bear is under one bureau and the black bear under another, and yet no one is able to define whether *a* brown bear may be *the* brown bear referred to in any particular instance. Four departments could pass on the lease of an island for fox farming. Cases have been noted where three years were taken to patent an uncontested claim or homestead, during which the papers made two round trips from Washington, D. C., to Alaska. The town of Valdez took thirteen years to get a town site approved. Secretary Work, in 1925, attacked Alaskan bureaucracy and lack of power by officials. Hoover said that Americans made about as bad a job of governing Alaska as they could if they had set out to do their worst. There is no single head to develop Alaska—hence, it does not develop. The federal and territorial governments overlap and duplicate one another and the finances of the two are mixed both in collections and expenditures. Alaska needs a systematic budget; it needs intelligent local advice for governmental officers in Washington; above all it needs coöperative effort toward solving the difficult problem of where and how government may best be the servant of the prosperous future of the territory.

The third great factor in Alaska's future—the question of capital—is chiefly one of when and how money will be attracted to Alaska in sufficient quantities to develop the territory properly. The sole factor in determining this would seem to be when the point of saturation for big profits in the United States has been reached. In other words, Alaska will not attract capital until the intervening territory of the United States has exhausted the possibilities of quick and easy return on invested funds. This will come when Alaska has a close and large market for her resources along the Pacific Coast. When that time arrives capital will be attracted to the territory and that day will bring competition to dissipate the present real or fancied evils of monopoly.

Along with the question of the future of capital in Alaska comes the question of settlers. If we consider that Alaska has superior advantages to northern Europe which supports a population of many millions, it is hard to conceive why the country has failed to attract Finlanders and Scandinavians. The chief reason for this failure is probably the great distance involved in such a migration. To overcome this handicap artificial stimulation such as that employed successfully by Canada must be resorted to. Scientists maintain that the best temperature for men to work in is that between 55 degrees and 70 degrees and that the best brain work is done when the outside temperature is around 40 degrees—hence, much of Alaska is ideally located. A moist climate is also ideal for man's needs. As for the polar regions, Rudmose Brown, the British geographer says: "The white races must turn, as in effect they have been turning for several centuries, polewards, in their search for new homes." The false impressions as to Alaska's temperature and other climatic conditions will be eradicated with the progress of education. The true advantages of the country for prospective home builders will then become apparent and the settlement of the territory should follow as a matter of course.

Previous to that date, the history of Alaska must certainly be one of speculation. It is conceivable, and in many ways logical, that the territory should be divided, as President Harding suggested after his trip to Alaska. Certainly the interests of southeastern Alaska are very different from those of the rest of Alaska, and the interests of southwestern Alaska almost as different again from those of the Yukon Valley. Whether these distinctions will be recognized by Congress, and in what way, is one of the problems for the future to work out. Alaska has the population to-day to warrant statehood, but sober-minded Alaskans do not wish this, as the cost of statehood would be almost prohibitive to them at the present time.

Alaska has suffered in the past from false ideas as to her resources. These were of two opposite kinds—first, the idea that Alaska had no resources, and then the equally bad impression that Alaska had unlimited resources. It would seem now as though both of these false impressions have been largely dissipated. It is wrong to say that Alaska is in any sense of the word to decline in the future. Her growth has been healthy as compared with that of any other pioneer country in the world. Compare the growth of the United States, located in a more temperate zone, between 1492 and 1677, when it was merely a collection of coastwise settlements with all interests and control centered in Europe; or Canada, whose population was no greater than Alaska's, when acquired by England. Alaska, between 1741 and 1926, has certainly progressed as much as the parent country did in the same period of growth, and there is no reason to believe that her proportionate growth will be any the less successful in the future.

INDEX

A'Court, Captain, commissioned by British government to maintain law and order in Alaska, 90.

Agriculture, future prospects of, in the Yukon Valley, 16; future growth, 21; development of resources, 178-180; government experimentation with soil, 180.

Ahtena Indians, hostility toward early explorers, 25; present population, 26.

Airplane, importance of, as means of transportation in Alaska, 185.

Alaska, its place in the history of North America, 1-3; area, 2; compared with that of United States, 2; map, 3; latitude, compared with Scandinavia, 4; scenic beauty of southeastern, 5; northern boundaries, 7; coast line, 7-8; characterization of Seward's purchase, 13; resources, 17-21; ethnology, Ch. II, 22-31; aboriginal inhabitants, 22; Indian population, 1890 and 1900, 30-31; discovery and explorations, Ch. III, 32-49; date of discovery, 35; meaning of, 35; Russian occupation, Ch. IV, 50-59; typical life in, under the Russians, 56; purchase of, by the United States, Ch. V, 60-80; events leading up to purchase, 66ff; fictitious sale to American Russian Company, 68; sale of, agitated by Constantine in 1866, 70; Seward's offer of purchase price, 72; actual purchase date and price, 72-73; events in Congress following purchase, 74; charges of bribery in connection with, 75-77; Seward's reasons for purchase, 79; reign of corruption and lawlessness, Ch. VI, 81-97; territorial government and administration, 83ff, Ch. IX, 129-140; governmental control by bureaus, 134-135, chart, 136, 188-192; the gold rush era, Ch. VII, 98-115; international complications, Ch. VIII, 116-128; causes of retarded growth, 140-141; social and intellectual growth, Ch. X, 142-155; histories and literature relating to, 153-154; economic development, Ch. XI, 156-180; modern development, Ch. XII, 181-191; present need for industrial development, 183; factors retarding growth, 183-192; misgovernment, 188-189; physical growth, compared to United States and Canada for similar periods, 191-192.

Alaska Commercial Company, organization, 72; holdings, 92; and the fur-seal industry, 172-174.

Alaska Pacific Fisheries, 164.

Alaska Packers' Association, 164.

Alaska Steamship Company, control of, 138, 160.

Alaska Syndicate, 137.

Alaskan Boundary Commission, personnel and work of, 120-121. See also *Boundary.*

Alaskan Gold Mining Company, 111.

INDEX

Alaskan Railroad Commissions, 185.
Aleut Indians, area inhabited by, 22; early population, 24; effect of Russian occupation on, 24; intermarriage with Russians, 24.
Aleutian Islands, easy access to Alaska by way of, 1, 4; extent and fertility of, 7; exploited by Russian traders, 40, 42.
Aleutian Peninsula, climate of, compared to New England, 14, 82.
Alexander Archipelago, coast line of, 7; geological character, 18.
Alexander the First, as promoter of new exploration of Alaska, 43; as stockholder in Lebedoff Company, 51; Napoleon's influence on, 58-60.
All-Alaska sweepstakes, Seppala as winner of, 150.
Allan, A. A., and dog racing in Alaska, 149-150.
American Russian Company, fictitious sale of Alaska to, 68.
Amundsen, Roald, successful search for Northwest Passage, 45.
Anderson, F. B., and regulation of fishing in Alaska, 169.
Andrews, C. L., *Sitka,* 56*n*.
Anglicanism, beginnings of, in Alaska, 30.
Anglo-Russian trade, effect of Northwest Passage on, 44.
Anian Strait, 34.
Anne, Empress, and Bering's explorations, 38.
Annette Island, and Tsimpshian Indians, 22, 27.
Annexation, American policy toward, 80.
Anvil Creek, 111.
"Apostle of Alaska," 146.
Appleton, and the purchase of Alaska, 69.
Arctic Brotherhood, organization of, 144-145.
Arctic slope, as continuation of Great Plains Region, 5.
Army rule, 85-90. See also *Navy Rule.*
Asia, Seward Peninsula as nearest point to, 8; crossed by Russians in 17th century, 33; and America proven to be separate continents, 35.
Astor, John Jacob, establishes Astoria, 48; enters into commercial agreement with Baranof, 53.
Astoria, 48.
Athapascan Indians, area inhabited by, 22.
Atlantic cable, effect on Collins' overland scheme, 64.
Aylesworth, A. B., appointed to Alaskan Boundary Commission, 120.

"Baldy," famous sled dog, 150.
Ball, M. D., failure to receive attention at Washington, 95.
Ballaine, John E., and government control of railroads in Alaska, 185.
Ballinger, Richard A., and Alaskan conservation, 138-139.
Ballinger-Pinchot controversy, 138.
Bancroft, H. H., 154.
Banks, General N. P., and the Alaskan Purchase, 74; and Alaskan bribery, 75.
Baranof, Alexander A., and importation of Aleuts into Sitka, 26; and Russian exploitation of Alaska, 43; and Russian occupation, 50-54; death of, 54.
Baranof Castle, 56.
Baronovich, C. V., 66.
Beach, Rex, and Nome Beach, 110; *The Spoilers,* 155; *The Iron Trail,* 155.

INDEX

Beardslee, Captain L. A., and provisional government, 90; effects co-operation from Chilkat Indians, 100. See also *Navy Rule.*
Bears, species, 143.
Beechy, Captain F. W., explorations of, 45.
Bering, Vitus, landing place of, 7; and discovery of Alaska, 33-36; voyages and explorations, 36-42; death of, 36, 40; maps of first and second voyages of, 37, 39; accomplishments of, compared to those of Columbus, 41.
Bering River oil fields, 163.
Bering Sea, non-existence of glaciers in, 6; Fur Seal Controversy, 123ff.
Bering Strait, the Diomede Islands and, 8.
Billings, J., 35; scientific expedition of, 152-153.
"Black Stream." See *"Kuro Siwo."*
Blaine, James G., and the Alaskan Purchase bribery, 77.
Booth Fisheries, 164.
Boston traders, mentioned by De Fonte, 46.
Boundary, Alaskan, as defined by English treaty of 1825, 116-118.
Brady, John G., removed as governor of Alaska, 130-131; 146.
Brandeis, Justice L. D., and Alaskan conservation, 139.
Bright, John, 73.
Bristol Bay, 11.
British Columbia, discovery of gold in, 98.
Brobdingnag, 155. See also *Swift.*
Brooks, A. H., on the mineral wealth of Alaska, 162, 183-184.
Brown, Rudmose, 190.
Buchanan, President James, and the Purchase of Alaska, 69.
"Bull Moose" Party, Alaska's influence on the organization of, 139.
Burke, Judge E., as member of fur company organized by Goldstone, 71.

Cables, submarine, failure of England's attempts to lay, 62.
Cale, T., Alaskan delegate to Congress, 132.
California, Russia's interests in, purchased by John A. Sutter, 55; discovery of gold in 1849, 98.
Canada, boundary line between Alaska and, 117ff.
Canning industry, development of, 165, 170-171.
Cape Camaano, 49.
Cape Lisburne, resources of, 19; coal fields, 160.
Cape Prince of Wales, 45.
Cape Spencer, 4.
Capital, necessity of, in the modern development of Alaska, 189-192.
Capitalism, 138.
Carmack, George, accepted discoveries of Klondike, 100-101.
Cassiar strike, 10; region, 66.
Catherine, Empress, and Bering's explorations, 38; and Russian expansion, 58.
Catholic Church, establishment of, in Alaska, 145.
Catholics, as religious leaders in Alaska, 30.
Central plateau, drainage of, 11.
"Cheechackos," 99.
Chilkat Indians, 26, 100.
Chilkoot Pass, 2, 10, 100.
Chinese labor, exclusion of, 94, 149; employment of, in fisheries, 165.
Chirikoff, Lieutenant Alexis, as Commander of the "St. Paul," 38; discovery of Alaska by, 40.

INDEX

Choquette, "Buck," discoveries of gold by, 66, 98-99.
Chugach Forest, 19.
Chukchi Indians, treatment of, by the Russians, 33-34.
Citizenship, 28; under the treaty of purchase, 85-86; granted to natives in 1915 by legislative act, 135.
Civil code, adoption of (1900), 114.
Civil government, army control of, 86ff.
Civilization, effect on pioneer life, 127-128, 146.
Claim jumping, at Nome, 109.
Clarence Strait. See *Portland Channel.*
Cleveland Peninsula, 49.
Climate and geography, Ch. I, 1-21; compared to European countries in same latitudes, 4; range of, 4; erroneous ideas concerning, 12-14; compared to northwestern part of United States, 13; disadvantages of, 14; "Kuro Siwo" as controlling element of, 14; compared to Washington, D. C., 15.
Coal, regions, 18, 160-161; quantity production compared to Pennsylvania, West Virginia and Ohio, 18; first mine at Port Graham, 66; attempts of federal government to create a monopoly in, 137; control of land by private concerns removed by President Roosevelt, 137, 138; the Cordova Party, 139-140; governmental restrictions on mining of, 160; present average production, 161-162.
Cold Bay, as center of future oil industry, 18, 163.
Cole, Senator Cornelius, and purchase of Alaska, 71, 73-74; relation to shareholders of Alaska Commercial Company, 92.
Collins, Percy McD., and plans for transcontinental telegraph system, 62-63, 77-78.
Colonial government. See *Territorial Government.*
Colorado, discovery of gold in, 98.
Columbus, Christopher, discoveries of, compared with Bering's, 41.
Commander Islands, Bering's ship wrecked on, 40.
Communication and travel, modern development of, 155ff.
Company land, 34.
Congressional representation, 114.
Connell, William A., organizes Arctic Brotherhood, 145.
Conservation, attitude of Alaskans toward, 131-140; President Roosevelt's policy of, 138.
Constantine, Grand Duke, and fictitious sale of Alaska, 68, 70.
Controller Bay, 7.
Cook and Vancouver expeditions, map, 47.
Cook, Captain James, 35; explorations of, 45.
Cook, Dr. F. A., alleged discovery of North Pole, 155.
Cook Inlet, non-existence of glaciers in, 6; most northern ice-free port, 7, 11; ideal climate of, 15.
Cooper, James Fenimore, 154.
Copenhagen, latitude, 4.
Copper, 10, 11; quantity production compared to that in Montana and Arizona, 18; annual production, 159-160.
Copper River, 7; and the Northwestern Railroad, 138.
Cordova Coal Party, 139-140.
Coronado, seven cities of, 34.
Corruption and lawlessness, reign of, Ch. VI, 81-97.
Cost of living, at Nome Beach, 110.
Courts, 129. See also *Police.*

INDEX

Crimont, Bishop, 30. See also *Seghers, Archbishop.*
Crosno, Frances, cited, 63*n.*
Cunningham, claims to Alaskan coal lands, legal dispute over, 138-139.
Customs laws, extended to Alaska, 89.

Dall, William H., 64, 154.
Darkness, range of, 17.
Darling, Mrs. E. B., and dog racing, 150.
Davis, General J. C., on Army Rule in Alaska, 86-87.
Davis, John, and the Northwest Passage, 44.
Dawson, gold routes to, 10.
De Fonte, Admiral, reported voyages of, 46.
De la Croyere, scientific observer on Bering's voyages, 38.
Deshneff, Simeon, and alleged discovery of Alaska, 33-35.
Diomede Islands, 8, 35.
Diphtheria epidemics, at Nome, 150-152.
Disasters at sea, due to lack of lighthouses, 147-148.
Dixon, Captain George, 45.
Dixon Entrance, 4, 49; establishment of Fort Simpson at, 57.
Dog racing, 149-150.
Doroshin, Peter, first miner under Russians, 56, 66.
Douglas, gold rush, 99.
Drainage, 10.
Duncan, Father William, and the Tsimpshian Indians, 27; as the "Apostle of Alaska," 29, 146.
Dunning, William A., cited, 75*n.*
Dyea, Canada's claims to port of, 118.

Edinburgh, geographical location, compared with Alaska, 4.
Education, development of, 153.
Elliott, Henry W., report on Alaska, 154.
Emerson, Ralph Waldo, and literature on Alaska, 155.
Endicott Range, 5, 9.
England, search for the Northwest Passage by, 44-45.
Epidemic, diphtheria, at Nome, 150-152.
Episcopal Church, early establishment of, 145.
Esquimaux, area inhabited by, 22; doubtful origin of, 22-23; physique, habits and occupation, 23; probable extinction of, 23; culture, 24; effect of civilization on, 24; vocabulary of language compared to that of college graduate, 27; Stefansson on difficulties of, 27; exploited by traders, 83.
Ethnology, Ch. II, 22-31.
Etolin, explorations of, 43.

Fairbanks, 10; gold field, 158, 162.
Farrand, Max, cited, 72*n.*
Feasts, ceremonials at, 26. See also *"Potlatch."*
Federal government of Alaska, control by bureaus, 134-135; chart, 136. See also *Territorial Government.*
Fiords, 5.
Fish, abundance of, 164; control of industry by trusts, 164; hatcheries, use of, 166.
Fisheries, growth and governmental restrictions on, 20, 163-172; Act of 1922, 169; Act of 1924, 170; monopoly, 138; exploited by private interests, 163-164; type of labor employed in, 165. See also *Whaling Industry.*
Forests, 19, 176-177; conservation, 138.

INDEX

Forney, Charles P., and Alaskan Purchase, 75.
Forty Mile Creek, discovered by Franklin, 100.
Fox farming, effect on fur industry, 20.
Fox furs, growing importance of, 174.
France, early Alaskan explorers, 46.
Franklin, Sir John and the Northwest Passage, 45; discovery of Forty Mile Creek by, 100.
Fraternities, 144-145.
Freight rates, excessive, 186-188.
Frobisher, Sir Martin, and the Northwest Passage, 44.
Fuca, Juan de, reported voyage of, 46.
Fur seal, effect of civilization on industry, 20; early Russian traders, 43; trade established between England and America, 48; Russia's inability to compete with other nations, 64-65; location of large herds, 124; breeding, 124-125; international dispute on protection of herds, 126-127; pelagic fishing for, 127-128; Japanese raid (1906), 127; partial depletion of resources due to monopoly, 172-173; international treaty, Dec. 15, 1911, 173-175; growth of industry under government control, 174.

Gama Land, 34.
Game laws, 143.
Games. See *Recreation.*
Gang rule, "Soapy" Smith, Frank Reid and, 106-107.
Gastineau mine, 159.
Geography and climate, Ch. I, 1-21; compared with European countries, 4.
Gilbert, Charles Henry, and regulations on fishing, 169.
"Gjoa," Amundsen's vessel, 45.
Glacier Bay, location and boundary, 5, 6, 122.
Glaciers, limited area of, 6; effect on boundary line of Alaska, 6, 122.
Glavis, W. R., and Alaskan conservation, 138-139.
Gold, discoveries, 10, 65-66, 93-94; era of, Ch. VII, 98-115; production, 18, 99ff.
Gold bearing districts, 10, 18, 66, 157ff.
Gold rush of 1899, Nome Beach and, 8.
Golder, F. A., on discovery of Alaska, 32; criticism of Deshneff, 34; *Purchase of Alaska,* 68*n*; motives of Russia during American Civil war, 70.
Goldstone, Louis, organizes fur company, 70-72.
Golikoff, 50.
Golovnin, V. M., 43.
Gorchakoff, Prince, opposed to sale of Alaska, 68.
Government of Alaska, by Federal bureaus, 188-189.
Governors, territorial, types of, 130.
Grant, President U. S., and the Alaskan Purchase bribery, 77; relations to Alaska Commercial Company, 92.
Gray, Captain, discovers the Columbia River, 46.
Great Plains Region, Arctic slope as continuation of, 5.
Great Salt Lake Region, 23.
Greek Church, permanent influence of, in Aleutian Islands, 29.
Guggenheims, financial investments of, in Alaska, 135-137; and interference with government control of railroads, 186.
Gwin, Senator W. McK., and purchase of Alaska, 69.

INDEX

Gwosdeff, M. S., and the alleged discovery of Alaska, 33, 35, 38.

Haida Indians, area inhabited by, 22, 26-27.
Halibut fishing, growth of, 171-172; Japanese as menace to, 172. See also *North Pacific Halibut Treaty* (1923).
Hall, C. F., and the Northwest Passage, 44.
Hanna, James, 46, 48.
Harbors, 5; effect of glaciers on the development of, 6-7.
Harding, President Warren G., and resources of Alaska, 17; visit to Alaska, 140, 169; on the division of Alaska, 191.
Harris, Dick, discovery of gold by, 93, 99.
Harrisburg, mining district of, 94.
Healey, coal region of, 18.
Henderson, Robert, discoverer of Klondike, 101-102.
Herman, Father, 29. See also *Juvenal, Father.*
Herring industry, 172.
H. M. S. "Alaska," and "Osprey" commissioned to maintain law and order in Alaska, 90.
History, and literature, works relating to Alaska, 153-154.
Hoggat, Wilfred B., as governor of Alaska, 137.
Holmes, Oliver Wendell, quoted, 69-70.
Holt, George, gold prospectings of, 100.
Holy Alliance, Russia's part in, 61.
Holy Cross, Jesuit mission established at, 30.
Holy Grail, search for, compared to that of Northwest Passage, 44.
Home rule, 132ff.
Home Rule Bill. See *Territorial Act* (1912).
Homestead laws (1903), 131.
Hoover, Herbert, sanctions regulations on fishing, 169.
Hough, Emerson, on the literature of Alaska, 155.
Howard, General O. O., on army rule, 87.
Hudson, Henry, and the Northwest Passage, 44.
Hudson Bay Company, 30; navigation of Yukon River by, 44; collides with Russian American Company, 54; lease of trading rights to Russian American Company, 57; union with Northwest Company, 65; dissolution of, 70.
Hunting, restrictions on, 143.
Hutchinson, Kohl and Company, purchase of Russian American Company holdings by, 92.

Ice, shipments to California (1855-1860), 56.
Icy Cape, 45.
Idaho, discovery of gold in, 98.
Imports, chief, 149.
Industries, Russia's attitude toward development of, 65-66, 156-157; monopolistic control, 92-94; growth of, 93.
Inland Empire, 4-5.
Inland Passage, scenic beauties of, 1, 5-6, 152.
Intellectual development, 152-153.
Intermarriage, 24, 31.
International complications, Ch. VIII, 116-127.
Inuits. See *Esquimaux.*
Irving, Washington, and the literature of Alaska, 155.
Islands, Aleutian, easy access to Alaska by way of, 1, 4, 40; extent and fertility, 7; exploited by

INDEX

Russian traders, 42, 124; Commander, Bering's ship wrecked on, 123; Diomede, 8, 35; Kayak, as the landing place of Bering, 7; Kodiak, annual temperatures at, 15; first school founded on, 153; Pribilof, as home of the seal, 20, 82; leased to Alaska Commercial Company, 92; government control of, 173. See also under name of Islands.

Ivy, Captain, 130*n*.

Jackson, Sheldon, 29-30; removal from office, 131, 146; imports first reindeer into Alaska, 177.

Japan, fur-seal raid (1906), 127.

Japan current. See *"Kuro Siwo."*

Japanese, as menace to halibut fishing, 172.

Jefferson, Thomas, and the Louisiana Purchase, 81-82.

Jesuits, mission at Holy Cross, 30.

Jette, Sir Louis, appointed to Alaskan Boundary Commission, 120.

Johnson, President Andrew, attitude toward purchase of Alaska, 72, 74-75; impeachment, 74.

Jordan, David Starr, and regulation of fishing, 169.

Judicial administration, provisions for (1884), 95ff; at Nome, 111.

Juneau, Joseph, discovery of gold by, 93, 99.

Juneau, gold rush, 94, 99; district, 158.

Juvenal, Father, and Father Herman, as Alaska's saints, 29.

Kaigani Indians, hostile to missionaries, 27.

Kake, 82.

Kamchatka, Russian explorations (1713), 33, 36.

Karta Bay, 66.

Kasaan, 82.

Kayak Island, landing place of Bering, 7.

Kenai Peninsula, 7.

Kennecott, Major Robert, 64.

Kennecott Mine, 49, 159, 162.

Ketchikan, failure of missionaries at, 29.

Keystone Canyon episode, 137.

Khotana Indians, adoption of Esquimaux traits by, 26.

"King of the Klondike," Alexander MacDonald as, 105.

Kinkead, John, first governor of Alaska, 130.

Kipling, Rudyard, quoted, 81.

Klawack, 82; first fish cannery established at, 164.

Klondike, fallacies regarding location, 1; Chilkoot Pass and, 10; discovery of gold in, 11, 12; effect of, 97; stampede to, 102-105; routes to, 102-106; gold production, 104-105; place in Alaskan history, 105; exhaustion of gold supply at, 111.

Knight, and the Northwest Passage, 44.

Kodiak, first school established at, 153.

Kodiak Island, 5; as center of future oil industry, 18; permanent settlement of fur traders on, 43; town, 82.

Koloshians, 83.

Kolyma, voyage of Deshneff from, 34.

Kotzebue Sound, 49.

"Kuro Siwo" (Japan Current), as controlling element in Alaska's climate, 14.

Kuskokwim, interior explorations of, by Lieutenant Nashilef, 44.

Kuskokwim delta, 9.

INDEX

Kutchin Indians, warlike nature of, 25.

Labor conditions, 143.
Lakes, 11. See also under names of Lakes.
Land laws, need for, 114.
"Land of Glaciers," 6.
Land titles, 131.
La Perouse, J. F. de G., and French explorations, 46.
Lapland, importations of reindeer from, 20-21.
Lawlessness, reign of, 83-91, 115.
Lebedoff Company, operations of, 51-52.
Legislation, Congressional (1884-1898), 97.
Legislative powers, limitations on, 133-134.
Lenin Land, 16.
Libby, D. B., and Nome gold rush, 107.
Lighthouses, dangers encountered from lack of, 147-148.
Liquor, illegal traffic in, 90-91, 148. See also *Prohibition.*
Lode mining, 159, 162.
Lodge, Henry Cabot, appointed to Alaskan Boundary Commission, 120.
Lomen Company, reindeer and, 177.
London, Jack, misleading description of Alaskan climate by, 13; cited, 127; and stories about Alaska, 154-155; *Sea Wolf,* 155.
Louisiana Purchase, Thomas Jefferson and, 81-82.
Lumber industry, 19. See also *Forests.*
Lynn Canal, 5, 100; Canada loses claim to, 121.

MacDonald, Alexander, as the "King of the Klondike," 105.
MacDonald, J. L., and fishing rights in Washington territory, 72.
Malakoff, Lieutenant, interior explorations by, 43-44.
Malaspina Glacier, 49.
Marine life, 146-147.
Mark Twain, and the literature of Alaska, 155.
Matanuska coal region, 18, 161.
McDonald, Robert (Archdeacon), 145.
McGrath, town, 11.
McKenzie, Alexander, and judicial corruption at Nome, 111-112; arrest and conviction, 112.
McLean, Abe, and the Japanese seal raid, 127; as London's character in the *Sea Wolf,* 155.
McPherson, Fort, average temperature at, 14.
Meares, Captain John, 45.
Mexico, Wrangell's negotiations with, for sale of land at Fort Ross, 55.
Miller, Joaquin, and literature of Alaska, 155.
Mineral wealth, 94, 162.
"Miner's law," administration of, 97.
Mining, early attempts at, 56; industry, 93-94, 156-163.
Missionaries, 27-29; obstacles to work of, 30; encouraged by Baranof, 63; Episcopal, 64.
Missions, 145-146.
Monopoly, of industries and transportation, 137ff; in gold and copper mining, 160.
Monroe Doctrine, 61.
Morgan, J. P., and Guggenheim brothers, attempts of, to control all sources of profit in Alaska, 138.
Mormons, projected migration to Alaska, 68.
Morris, W. G., report on Alaska, 154.

Mount McKinley National Park, 151.
Mountain passes, 8-9.
Mountain system, harbors and islands formed by, 5.
Mountains, as barrier to early explorations, 2; Logan, 4, 9; McKinley, 4, 9; St. Elias, 4, 40; Wrangell, 4; Endicott range, 9; Aleutian, 9.
Moving pictures, 149.
Muller, G. F., on Deshneff's voyage, 34.
Munchausen, Baron, 155.

Napoleon, and the Russian navy occupation of Alaska, 58; influence on Alexander I, 60.
Napoleon III, and Russia's opposition to intervention in the American Civil war, 69.
Nasilef, Lieutenant, interior explorations of, 44.
Navigable rivers, 10-11. See also under name of river.
Navigation, dangers of early, 146-147; modern aids to, 148.
Navigators, early English, 44-45.
Navy Rule, 90. See also *Army Rule.*
Neglect, Ch. VI, 81-97.
Nenana coal mine, 161.
New Mexico, discovery of gold in, 98.
Nicholas, J. P., *Constitutional History of Alaska,* 130*n*.
Nome, lowest recorded temperature, 15-16; discovery of gold in, 98, 107-108; government by miners, 198ff.
Nome Beach, gold rush (1899), 8, 109-110.
Nootka Sound, types of English and Spanish navigators at, 46; Controversy (1789-95), 61.
North Cape, latitude, 4.
North Pacific Halibut Treaty (1923), 172. See also *Halibut Fishing.*
North Pacific Sealing Convention, 127-128.
North Pole, alleged discovery by Dr. Cook, 155.
Northwest Company, established by John Jacob Astor, 48; united with Hudson Bay Company, 65. See also *Hudson Bay Company.*
Northwest Passage, Sir Martin Frobisher and, 44; early explorations for, 44-45; discovery by Roald Amundsen, 45.
Novidiskoff, Michael, 43.
Novo Zemla, 34.
Noyes, Judge A. H., judicial corrupt practices of, 111-112; arrest and conviction, 112-113; as portrayed by Rex Beach, 155.
Nulato, 44.

Occupation, Russian, Ch. IV, 50-59.
Oil, regions, 18; quality and production, 163.
Omalik, 107.
Ophir Creek, discovery of gold in, 108.
Oregon, United States claim to, 61-62; laws of, applicable to Alaska by Act of 1884, 114.
Organic Law (1884), 95, 131-132.

Pacific Packing and Navigation Company, 164.
Pepper, Senator G. W., and Alaskan conservation, 139.
Perkins, Benjamin, claims against United States government, 76-77. See also *Alaskan Purchase.*
Peter the Great, commissions Bering's expedition, 36, 41; and Russian expansion, 58.
Petroff, Ivan, and the census of

Alaska, 113; report on Alaska, 154.
Petroleum v. *Naseby,* quoted, 78.
Philippine Islands, purchase, maintenance and cost compared to Alaska, 187.
Pierce, President Franklin, 63*n.*
Pinchot, Gifford, as chief forester of Alaska, 138; attitude of Alaskans toward conservation policy of, 139-140.
Pioneer Mining Company, 111.
Pioneers of Alaska, organization of, 145.
Placer mining, 157-159, 162. See also *Lode Mining.*
Plateaus, 9.
Poetry, Alaskan, 154.
Point Barrow, latitude, 4; lowest recorded temperature, 15; resources, 19; named by Captain Beechy, 45; coal field, 160.
Police, inadequacy of, 128. See also *Courts.*
Political history (1895-1919), 131ff.
Politics, beginnings of, 131ff.
Polk, President F. K., and Oregon claim, 61-62.
Popoff, Admiral, mention of Alaska by, 35; and sale of Alaska, 69.
Population, Indian, (1890 and 1900), 30-31; (1867), 82, 113; (1880, 1890, 1900), 113-114; (1910 and 1920), 181; effect of World War on decrease of, 182.
Port Graham, first coal mine established at, 66.
Port Tongass, 82.
Portland Channel, 5; boundary line, 121.
Portland Oregonian, Jan. 13, 1907, cited, 69*n.*
Portlock, Captain, 45.
"Potlatch," 26. See also *Feasts.*
Poverty, non-existence of, 143.
Presbyterians, early missionary work of, 29; end of hierarchy rule in Alaska by, 131; establish church, 146.
Pribilof Islands, as home of the seal, 20; leased to Alaska Commercial Company, 92; government control of, 173.
Prince of Wales Island, 5, 22, 117.
Prince William Sound, as center of future and extreme beauty, 7; landing place of Bering, 40.
Progressive Party, Alaska's influence in organization of, 139.
Prohibition, failure of, 89-91, 97; repealed, 114.
"Promishleniki," 33, 50.
Pulp, and timber industry, 19, 175ff. See also *Lumber Industry.*

Quadra, Bodega, voyages of, 46.
Quadra Bay, 49.
Quay, Matthew S., 130.
Queen Charlotte Sound, 26-27.
Quicksilver, discovery of, in Kuskokwim River basin, 19.

Races, of Alaska, Ch. II, 22-31.
Radio, 155.
Railways, White Pass, 10; early objections to, 95; site of first Klondike, 106; governmental development, 140, 184-187.
Rainfall, 15.
Raven, as clan symbol of Thlingit tribe, 26.
Recreation, types of, 149.
Reid, Frank, end of gang rule by, 107.
Reindeer, number and importance of, 20-21; introduced into Alaska, 131; importations and growth, 177-178.
Religion, 145. See also *Missionaries. Missions.*

INDEX

Ripinsky, Colonel Sol, and the Chilkat Indians, 100.
Representation, in Congress, 132.
Resources of Alaska, 17-21; conservation of, 156ff. See also *Agriculture. Gold. Fisheries. Fur Seal. Mining.*
Resurrection Bay, 7.
Revenues, compared to other United States dependencies, 131.
Reynolds-Alaska Development Company, 137.
Riggs, Governor Thomas, on need for increased police protection, 129-130.
Rivers, Anadir, 34; Cassiar, discovery of gold in, 98; Chilkat, 10; Columbia, discovery of, by Captain Gray, 46; Copper, 10; Fish, 107; Fraser, discovery of gold in, 98; Klondike, 12; Koyukuk, 12; Kuskokwim, 9, 19, 66; Lewes, 100; Nass, 27; Peace, 23; Skeena, 27; Stewart, 100; Stikine, 10; establishment of fort near mouth of, 57; English expedition to, stopped by Russians in 1883, 65; first gold strike made on, 66; Sushitna, 11; Taku, 10; Tanana, 10, 12; Yukon, 9, 10, 11, 30, 44; its importance in the development of Alaska, 12; explored by Lieutenant Schwatka, 89.
Roosevelt, Theodore, and North Pacific Sealing Convention, 128; removes John G. Brady as governor of Alaska, 130-131; and Alaskan representation in Congress, 131; and conservation policy, 138; and "Bull Moose" Party, 139; made honorary life member of Arctic Brotherhood, 145.
Root, Elihu, appointed to Alaskan Boundary Commission, 120.
Ross, Fort, establishment of factory at, by Baranof, 52.
"Rough Necks," 137.
Rousseau, General Lovell H., Alaska formally turned over to, 74.
Rowe, Bishop Peter Trimble, 30, 145.
Russia, abuse of Aleut Indians by early traders of, 24; establish settlement in Sitka (1802), 26; and the discovery of Alaska, 33; claims to Alaska, 42; actual exploration of Alaska by, 42; occupation of Alaska by, Ch. IV, 50-59; friendly attitude during Civil War, 69.
Russian America, encroachment of other nations on, 64.
Russian American Company, conflict with Hudson Bay Company, 54; lease of trading rights to Hudson Bay Company, 57; failure to renew charter, 58, 64-65; granted a monopoly in Karta Bay, 66; abuses by, 67, 70; sale of holdings to Hutchinson, Kohl and Company, 92.
Russian expansion, spread and collapse of, 58.
Russian Orthodox Church, work of, 145.

"St. Gabriel," Bering's ship, used by Gwosdeff, 38.
"St. Paul," Lieutenant Chirikoff as the commander of, 38.
"St. Peter," Bering's ship on second voyage, 38.
Salmon fishing, history and growth, 165; attempts at conservation, 166; traps for catching, illustration, 167, 168.
Salmon industry, effect on people of Alaska, 27-28; growth, 93; ex-

port figures for 1918 and 1921 compared, 182.
Saloons, early prevalence of, 148, See also *Prohibition.*
Sandwich Islands, proposed seizure by Baranof, 52.
"Santa Maria" size of, compared to Bering's vessels, 42.
Saxman, failure of missionaries at, 29.
Schools, in Kodiak and Sitka, 67. See also *Education.*
Schwatka, Lieutenant Frederick, explorations of, 89.
Sea Otter, partial extinction of, 175.
Seal, home of the, 20. See also *Fur Seal. Pribilof Islands.*
Seghers, Archbishop Charles J., and Bishop Crimont as Jesuit leaders, 30, 146.
Seppala, Leonhard, and the diphtheria epidemic at Nome, 150-152.
Service, Robert W., false description of Alaskan climate by, 13; and poetry on Alaska, 154; *Spell of the Yukon,* 154; *The Cremation of Sam McGhee,* 154; *The Shooting of Dan McGrew,* 154.
Seward, William H., and the purchase of Alaska, 13, 69, 72, 79; on fishing rights in Alaska, 72; quoted, 78.
Seward Peninsula, resources, 19; forests of, 20; site of Russian explorations, 1761-1775, 43; discovery of gold on, 107.
"Seward's Ice Box," 81.
Shakes, Chief, as slave holder, 26; death of, 26.
Shamanism, 23.
Sheakley, John, as governor of Alaska, 130.
Shelikoff, Grigor, 50-51, 54; founded first school in Alaska, 153.
Shipwrecks, causes of, 147-148.
Siberia, access to Alaska from, 1; difficulties of possible railway traffic with, 8.
Simpson, Fort, established by the English, 57.
Sitka, geographic location, 4; rainfall and temperature, 15; settled by Russia in 1802, 26; landing place of Chirikoff, 40; Baranof, 53, 82.
Sitka-Wrangell feud, 26.
Skagway, 10; gang rule at, 106-107; Canada's claims to port of, 118.
Skating, and coasting, limited season for, 15.
Skookum, Jim, companion of Carmack, 101.
Slavery, as practiced by the Thlingits, 25-26.
Smith, Jefferson R., ("Soapy") gang rule of, 106-107.
Snowfall, 15.
Social and intellectual growth of Alaska, Ch. X, 142-155. See also *Education.*
Society, abnormal growth of, 144.
"Sonora," Quadra's ship, 46.
"Sourdoughs," 12, 100.
Spain, early Alaskan explorations of, 45-46.
Spanish War, effect on Klondike stampede, 103.
Spicer, G. W., *Status and Government of Alaska,* 96*n*.
Sports. See *Recreation. Social and Intellectual Growth.*
Sprague, A. J., 166*n*.
Standard Oil Company, effect on whaling industry, 20, 171.
Stanton, and Alaskan bribery, 75.
State Island, 34.
Stefansson, V., on the climate of Alaska, 14; on the true nature of Alaska, 17; on the Esquimaux language, 27.

INDEX

Steller, G. W., and Bering's discoveries, 38, 40; scientific contributions to Alaska, 152.

Stevens, Thaddeus, and the Alaskan purchase, 74-75.

Stick Indians, 100.

Stoeckl, Baron Edward de, 63*n*; and sale of Alaska, 68, 70; quoted, 75.

Stuck, Archbishop, 145.

Sumner, Charles, 67*n*; effect of personal influence on the purchase of Alaska, 73, 154.

Sunlight, unequal distribution of, 14, 17.

Sutherland, Dan, as Alaskan delegate in Congress, 132; opposed to regulations on fishing, 169.

Sutter, John A., purchases Russia's interests in California, 55.

Swift, Jonathan, *Gulliver's Travels,* cited, 155.

Swineford, Governor, and Chinese pioneers, 94; as governor, 130.

Tabu, 23.

Tacitus, unknown north of, 16.

Taft, William Howard, recommends government railways for Alaska, 140.

Tagish, Charles, companion of Carmack, 101.

Tanana, gold field, 159.

Taxation, and representation, 131.

Telegraph, Collins' overland plan, 62-63, 64, 78. See also *Cables.*

Temperature, 14-15; compared to other countries, 15-16.

Terra de Jeso, 34.

Territorial Act (1912), 132-133.

Territorial Bill (1913), effect on conservation, 140.

Territorial government and administration, 83ff, Ch. IX, 129-141.

Thlingit Indians, area inhabited by, 22; warlike attitude toward early Russian settlers, 26.

Thompson Pass, 2, 10.

Timber and pulp industry, 175ff. See also *Forests.*

Tongass, Fort, temperature at, 15; forest, 19, 177.

Totem poles, symbolism of, 26, 30, 31.

Tourists, Alaska as an attraction for, 151-152.

Town government, administration of, 130. See also *Territorial Government.*

Towns, present growth, 143-144.

Trade jargons, 27.

Trade treaty between Russia and United States (1824), 54-56; closed to foreign countries by ukase of 1821, 60-61.

Trading companies, Hudson Bay and Northwest Company, 48; Russian, 50-53; American, 54; English, 54; friction between Russian, English and American, 54. See also under names of companies.

Transportation, railway, 183-187; water, 187-188; excessive rates of, 186-188.

Travel routes, 63-65.

Treadwell, John, purchase of gold interests by, 99.

Treadwell mine, 99, 159, 162.

Treaties (1884), violation of, by Russians, 65; boundary, 116-123; fur, 123-128.

Tsimpshian Indians, area inhabited by, 22; government reservation for, on Annette Island, 27; and William Duncan, 29.

Tuberculosis, cause for prevalence of, 28.

Tundra, location of, 8.

INDEX

Turner, George, appointed to Alaskan Boundary Commission, 120.

Unalaska, heavy rainfall at, 15, 82.
Unimak Island, fertility of, 7.
United States, first attentions to Alaska, 46-47; purchase of Alaska by, Ch. V, 60-80; President's Commission on Criminal Law and Procedure, appointment of, 114; Secretary of Commerce, granted authority to limit fishing (Act of 1924), 170.
U. S. S. "Jamestown" commissioned to maintain law under Navy Rule, 90.
U. S. S. "Shenandoah," arctic cruise of, 62.
Ural Mountains, crossed by Russians, 33.

Valdez, 10; temperature at, 15; "Pathfinder," 101*n*.
Vancouver, George, importance of explorations of, 45; and voyages with Quadra, 46.
Vegetation, 16.
Veniaminoff, Bishop Innocent, missionary work of, 24, 29, 145.
Von Kotzebue, Otto, explorations of, 43.
Von Krusenstern, Captain A. J., sent on world voyage by Alexander the First, 43.

Wages, standards of, 143.
Walker, R. J., quoted, 67-68; and Alaskan bribery, 75.
"Walrussia," 81.
Washington, D. C., temperature of, compared with southeastern Alaska, 15.
Washington Historical Quarterly, 72*n*.
Washington Territorial Act (1853), 133.
Waskey, F. H., Alaskan delegate in Congress, 132.
Western Union Telegraph Company, adopts Collins' transcontinental plan, 63; expedition (1863), 107.
Weymouth, and Northwest Passage, 44.
Whaling industry, disappearance of, 20; evils introduced by, 24; America's entry into, 57; effect of Civil War on, 62; growth and decline, 62, 93, 171.
Whiskey, love of natives for, 83. See also *Prohibition*.
White Pass, 100, 152.
White Pass Railway, 10.
Wickersham, Judge James, appointed to succeed Judge Noyes, 113; as Alaskan delegate in Congress, 132, 137.
Wild Goose Mining Company, 111.
Wilkins, Captain Hubert, flight of, 48-49.
Wilson, Woodrow, government railway started under administration of, 139-140.
Wireless, 155.
"Woewod," as governor of Siberia, 34.
Wolf tribe, as clan of Thlingits, 26.
World War, effect on Alaskan bitterness toward conservation, 140; effect on the population of Alaska, 182.
Wrangell Island, 49, 54, 57, 82, 87-88; town, 26, 35.

Yakutat, 82.
Yakutat Bay, 7.
Young, S. Hall, 29, 146.

INDEX

Yukon, delta, 9; fort, established by Hudson Bay Company, 57; territory, effect on Alaskan colonial administration, 140-141; valley, agricultural prospects of, 16; forests, 19; river, navigation on, 10-12; mineral resources of, 19. See also under *Rivers. Navigation.*

Zagoskin, interior explorations by, 43-44.

Zarambo, establishes fort at Wrangell, 57.